Defiant Women of Faith

Defiant Women of Faith

A Fifty-Two Week Devotional for Women Seeking To Live Authentically Free

Dr. Vanetta R. Rather

Explore How Fifty-Two Powerful Women in Scripture
Empower Contemporary Women to
Live in Abundant Freedom

ISBN-13: 9781979443838
ISBN-10: 1979443831

Contents

Entries

An Invitation To Authentic Freedom

As a woman of faith, a preacher, a strong advocate for women and girls, and one who is committed to walking confidently in this world, it's always a blessing when I find resources that encourage me on my journey. This devotional is meant to serve as another resource to help encourage women who are also on a similar journey.

Today I invite you on a journey to live the abundant life Jesus afforded us when he said, "I have come that they may have life, and that they have it more abundantly."

> *"I have come that they may have life,*
> *and that they have it more abundantly."*
> *(John 10:10, NKJV)*

Abundant life is not one size fits all. What one woman considers abundant living may be wildly different from how another woman envisions it. And exploring and finding what abundant living means for us as individuals is at the core of this devotional.

For too many years of my life I was, without realizing it, denying myself the abundant life Jesus said was available to me. Instead of living my life, I was living the life I was conditioned by family, culture, and faith traditions to live. But I was set free when I realized that who I thought I was and who I was conditioned to be were in conflict with who I was created to be—with who I sensed I was internally.

I, like so many other women I've encountered, was living this cookie-cutter life that was modeled for and taught to me. I was walking in steps not so much ordered by the Lord as they were ordered by the ideals set for women. But I soon realized that I couldn't become the woman God was designing me to be if I remained the woman I was conditioned to be. And this is when I began the journey to my abundant life.

My journey began when I unshackled myself from the opinions, expectations, and ideas others had for me and began to walk in my authenticity. My journey began when I decided to give myself permission to be the woman who I knew deep down inside God created me to be! When I decided to listen and follow more intently the internal voice over all of the external voices that continually tried to shape my identity, I began to experience a peace like never before and a confidence that was unshakable.

> *I couldn't be the woman God was designing me to be*
> *if I remained the woman I was conditioned to be.*

The decision to fully trust that the same God who spoke the world into existence was also speaking to me about my existence was life changing. Completely trusting my direct access and connection to God was the first liberating step on my journey. It was the step that gave me the fierce boldness to freely walk unmasked and unapologetic in this world.

Abundant living doesn't mean we live perfect lives. It means we live the lives best suited for us. This is what I desire for myself and for all women. I want women to be free to live the lives, make the decisions, and follow the paths that will be most fulfilling and rewarding. And this kind of freedom begins with God. It begins when women are able to view women in the Bible through a more empowered lens.

As a woman, I read and study scripture through my experience, and nothing has fueled my journey to live **authentically free** like the courageous women I've encountered in scripture. Studying these women and witnessing the righteous defiance that many of them displayed was the catalyst for change in my personal life, and I believe it can be the catalyst for other women braving this path.

So often women in the Bible are interpreted as passive and submissive, which is understandable when you take into account that they were oppressed, seen and treated as property, and had very few, if any, rights. But when we allow our gaze to penetrate beneath the surface of their stories, we are able to see a more compelling and empowering view of women in scripture. These women often challenged systems that oppressed them. They often made decisions and took risks to live lives that were more congruent with what they sensed internally, which serves as inspiration for modern women looking to do the same. Their witness helps contemporary women of faith, in very practical ways, break from traditions that don't foster liberation and that keep women shackled.

True liberation is what Jesus offers women, but in a world that doesn't listen too much to what Jesus says—a world that sees and treats women as the lesser gender—liberation must be fought for and won! Like women in scripture, women today have to fight against embedded beliefs and unlearn much of what we've been conditioned to believe about ourselves individually and collectively.

This devotional is designed to help in the fight by sharing liberating lessons gleaned from the defiant women of faith we encounter in scripture.

True liberation is what Jesus offers women!

When I mention the term "defiant women," it is often met with an unsettling response. Some aren't comfortable with women, especially women of faith, being defiant! Discomfort, however, is not necessarily a bad thing. Growth often stems from our places of discomfort.

What's important to remember is that these women didn't defy God; they defied the status quo and cultural norms of their day. In some cases, these women were used by God to confront, challenge, and disrupt the status quo. In other cases, these women were simply self-aware enough to understand when a situation necessitated defiance. What's also worth pointing out is that it seemed God didn't use these women in spite of their defiant attitude, but because of it.

Defiance is not a dirty word! I would argue that in some respects, it is the only appropriate response for women who are determined to live authentic and free in a world that is designed to keep women in a certain place. A little defiant faith is a requirement for women seeking to live the abundant, authentic lives Jesus afforded us!

So today I invite you to join me on this yearlong journey of becoming a **defiant woman of faith living in authentic freedom**!

How to Use This Devotional

This devotional was written to help women live more authentically free in every area of life. It touches on areas of faith, career, relationships, and sisterhood to help inspire women to embrace and be fully accepting of self.

There are fifty-two entries that each reflect on a woman in scripture. The fifty-two entries coincide with the year calendar, but don't feel compelled to follow this time line. Please use this devotional at your own pace. If you need to linger a week or two on an entry, do so! If you skip around the entries, not following in the order presented, that's fine too. The title of a particular entry may draw your attention, and it may be just what you need that week. Please feel free to jump around and find your own flow. There is a box next to each entry in the table of contents so you can keep track of entries you've read.

Each entry focuses on either one woman or a group of women in the Bible. Some are very familiar women, some are names we rarely hear, and some are nameless women. The goal of each entry is to see the woman/women through a new lens that allows her/their ancient story of empowerment to encourage us on our present journey. Each entry also includes the following:

- Broad Scripture Reference
- Focus Scripture Reference
- Meditation Thought
- Affirmation Statement

- Weekly Prayer
- Journal Notes

A "Me Time" Suggestion for Optimal Use

At the beginning of a seven-day span, find a quiet time to give yourself to complete the following steps.

1. Take a few moments to read the broad passage of scripture for context.
2. Reread the focus scripture and reflection.
    a. Think through the scripture and reflection and ask yourself:
        i. Does this woman of scripture resonate with you?
        ii. Does this reflection/passage interrupt a long-held view and/ or bring into question an embedded belief you've held about women in general and women in the Bible?
        iii. What is your internal voice saying to you about you as it pertains to this entry?
3. Read the meditation thought and sit in silence with it for a few moments. (There is no time limit to the meditation.)
4. Recite and rehearse the affirmation statement and use it to affirm yourself throughout the week.
5. Read the prayer and ask God's grace in helping you point out areas in your life where you need to be more authentic to ensure you are living in the freedom and abundance Jesus affords us.
6. On the last day of your seven-day span, take a few moments to journal some thoughts about this week's devotional lesson.

Week 1

Nameless Widow

When No Is Unacceptable

Luke 18

Scripture Focus

Then Jesus told his disciples a parable to show them that they should always pray and not give up. He said: "In a certain town there was a judge who neither feared God or cared what people thought. And there was a widow in that town who kept coming to him with the plea, Grant me justice against my adversary. For some time he refused. But finally he said to himself, 'Even though I don't fear God or care what people think, yet because this widow keeps bothering me, I will see that she gets justice, so that she won't eventually wear me out with her continual coming.'" And the Lord said, "Listen to what the unjust judge says. And will not God bring about justice for his chosen ones, who cry out to him day and night? Will he keep putting them off? I tell you, he will see that they get justice, and quickly. However, when the Son of Man comes, will he find faith on the earth?" (Luke 18:1–8, NRSV)

Scripture Reflection

My favorite of all the nameless women in the Bible—the one who inspires me to never settle and to be as courageous as I can—is this nameless widow in Luke's Gospel. She epitomizes what it means to be a defiant woman of faith. Jesus uses this woman as a model to teach his disciples, then and now, what relentless, tenacious faith looks like.

Jesus's parable is proof that women shouldn't always accept no as a final answer. His parable is further proof that if women are going to possess those things that are rightfully ours, we have to develop and employ persistent faith. As doors are slammed in our faces, denying us access to spaces we know we belong, persistence and faith become needed weapons.

Women throughout history have always had to fight for every inch of progress in the war for equality; in many instances, we've lost battles on our journey to win the war. But the question that I asked myself as I meditated on this passage was, "What made this nameless widow persevere after losing so many battles?" I wondered what it was that made her continue to come back after she consistently heard this judge—who held authoritative power over her—constantly tell her no? How was she able to keep coming back after so many rejections?

Rejection is a hard beast to overcome. Rejection makes us question if something is wrong with us! Rejection can make us think we don't have what it takes, that we aren't worthy, and that we aren't enough. But rejection didn't have this impact on this widow. She didn't take no for an answer, and we all need some of whatever it was that made her face rejection the way she did!

What kept this woman coming back, and what will help women today persevere in the face of rejection, is her ability to see the judge in the proper context. It is likely that this nameless widow kept coming back because she knew the judge's no wasn't the final word on her situation. She knew that there was another judge who was Judge over all judges! She must have believed that she was pursing something that belonged to her and that the God of Justice desired her to have it. Therefore, she never gave up!

This should encourage and remind women that a no is sometimes totally unacceptable. The judge didn't intend to give this woman the justice she was owed, but God used her persistent, tenacious faith as the vehicle to bring about change. This nameless woman reminds women that God can make people do for you what they had no intention of doing for you.

In this parable, Jesus equates this widow's tenacity with faith! Women need persistent faith to get what God has for us because the world and its systems are sometimes relentlessly opposed to women taking their rightful places.

This nameless widow reminds women to be persistent in pursing what we believe belongs to us.

Women who refuse to take someone's no as a final answer on what they believe belongs to them are women who will break down barriers meant to hold us back. These are women who are not only destined to live authentically free, but they, like this nameless widow, become models of inspiration to other women so they too can live free.

Meditation Thought

"Greatness is not measured by what a man or woman accomplishes, but by the opposition he or she has overcome to reach it."—Dorothy Height

Affirmation Statement

I refuse to quit, and I will not be distracted or turned away by the perceived powers others think they have over me!

Prayer

Dear Lord, this week help me to remember that you alone have the final say in my life, and you alone determine how far I go, how much I achieve, and the heights I climb. Help me remember that every no I get is merely a suggestion. Remind me that unless I get a no from you, I haven't really been told no!

Journal Reflections

_____
_____
_____
_____
_____
_____

Week 2

Achsah

Make Your Request Known

Joshua 15

Scripture Focus

And Caleb said, "Whoever attacks Kiriath-sepher and takes it, to him I will give my daughter Achsah as wife." Othniel son of Kenaz, the brother of Caleb, took it; and he gave him his daughter Achsah as wife. When she came to him, she urged him to ask her father for a field. As she dismounted from her donkey, Caleb said to her, "What do you wish?" She said to him, "Give me a present; since you have set me in the land of the Negev, give me springs of water as well." So Caleb gave her the upper springs and the lower springs. (Josh. 15:16–19, NRSV)

Reflection

There are times when women who speak up to get their needs met will be labeled as aggressive, demanding, or insubordinate. A woman merely asking for what she wants or needs can be seen as an act of aggression, as is the case with Achsah.

4

I found it interesting that Achsah is labeled "the Discontented Bride" in some commentaries that expound on her short story. She is described as the woman who didn't appreciate what she had been given. Apparently, her additional request to the dowry she had been given positioned her comfortably in the category of "those women who are never satisfied."

I have a different view of Achsah. I celebrate this woman for her courage to express her wants and needs.

In a time when women had no control over their lives, when women didn't have a say in who they married and how and where they lived, Achsah asserts her own voice to ensure the best possible outcome for her future. Achsah gives us a different glimpse of how women in biblical history weren't just passive bystanders when it came to how they lived. These women were proactive players who ensured they too received their share of the Promised Land.

Achsah had every intention of claiming her share in God's promise. But not only does she secure a piece of the promise for herself, this wise woman who is unafraid to use her voice secures what she needs to maintain the promise.

The land that would be hers and her husband's when she married was a dry land in the Negev. And if this land was to produce life-sustaining crops, she needed to also secure resources to water the land. Without this additional request, Achsah would not have had what was needed to flourish in the Promised Land. So she did what every woman today needs to do. She asked for what she needed to ensure her future was fruitful. Her request is not out of greed or some insatiable desire for more! Her request was prudent! It was self-caring! It was a request that articulated her needs.

Women should never be made to feel like we are asking too much when we are articulating our needs. Our needs, wants, and desires are worthy of being heard and accommodated. I'm sure that the men, and perhaps some women, of her day looked at Achsah and believed she was overstepping her role as a woman, wife, and daughter, but Achsah proves to women that if we stay in the boxes people have designed for us, we will never get to the places of promise God has for us!

No one can—and, more likely, no one will—articulate our needs like we can. In our places of work, ministries, academia, and in every area of life, women have to insist on our needs being met.

Women can't produce the lives God has promised us if we aren't willing to do what Aschsah did and make our requests known.

Women who are not afraid to articulate their needs are women who will have their needs met!

Meditation Thought
It's never an overreach to ask for what you want and need!

Affirmation Statement
I am worthy of what I desire and I will only get in life that which I have the courage to ask for, or at times, demand!

Prayer
Dear Lord, this week help me be mindful that if I don't go after what I desire, I will never have it. Remind me that if I don't ask for and/or demand what I truly desire, the answer will always be no. Help me to understand that if I don't step forward to claim what you said I can have, I can't receive all you have for me.

Journal Reflections

_____
_____
_____
_____
_____
_____
_____
_____
_____
_____
_____
_____
_____
_____

Week 3

Canaanite Woman

Tough-Skinned Faith

Matthew 15

Scripture Focus

Leaving that place, Jesus withdrew to the region of Tyre and Sidon. A Canaanite woman from the vicinity came to him, crying out, "Lord, Son of David, have mercy on me! My daughter is demon-possessed and suffering terribly." Jesus did not answer a word. So his disciples came to him and urged him, "Send her away, for she keeps crying out after us." He answered, "I was sent only to the lost sheep of Israel." The woman came and knelt before him. "Lord, help me!" she said. He replied, "It is not right to take the children's bread and toss it to the dogs." "Yes it is, Lord," she said. "Even the dogs eat the crumbs that fall from the master's table." Then Jesus said to her, "Woman, you have great faith! Your request is granted." And her daughter was healed at that moment! (Matt. 15:21-28, NIV)

Scripture Reflection

The story of the Canaanite woman is the passage that most reminds me of the tough skin a women of faith must possess.

I've learned over the years that faith is not for the faint of heart. Faith is not best suited for delicate, easily offended women. Faith is a brass-knuckles kind of business, and those who desire to walk by faith must have tough skin. Tough-skinned faith is sometimes required to acquire all we were meant to experience, and nothing makes this clearer than Jesus's tough-love encounter with the Canaanite woman.

So often Jesus is presented to us as this docile, lily-white, blue-eyed man who turns all of our rainy days into sunshine-filled skies, but this is not the Jesus I've come to know and love! The Jesus I know and love allows us to experience hurt and pain, he allows us to go through some very traumatic experiences, and he even seemingly, at times, ignores our desperate pleas for relief.

Jesus ignores the Canaanite woman when she cries, "Help me! My daughter is suffering terribly." And much like her, we have all at one point or another heard silence from Jesus when we've cried out for help! The Jesus we encounter in this passage is not the Savior we are used to seeing who loves healing and delivering those in need.

As I wrestled with this passage, I questioned why Jesus would treat her this way. But then I realized that in my own life, I've come to understand that Jesus is always more concerned about my development than what I desire of him. More than Jesus granting me things I desire of him, Jesus wants me to develop into who I'm called to be in him. This development sometimes requires silence, an answer of "no," or some other kind of uncomfortable, unwanted response.

There have certainly been times when we would prefer an easier path than the hard path Jesus has allowed us to take. But in hindsight, and when you realize that all things really do work for your good, like me, you'll always end up more grateful for the painful path. These difficult experiences in life strengthen us and make us tough!

I imagine this Canaanite woman had to make a similar journey on a very difficult path. Having a daughter who was demon-possessed had to have presented significant challenges that developed a strength inside of her she probably didn't know she had. By the time she encounters Jesus, her faith muscle had to have been exercised quite a bit. So I imagine that the harsh tone Jesus seems to take with her is more about Jesus showing her just how strong her faith was.

Faith is forged in the fire! Difficult experiences either show us how strong our faith is or how much we need to be strengthened in faith.

According to Jesus's words, "You have great faith," this Canaanite woman's faith was Teflon strong. Jesus had given her some harsh blows. He ignored and insulted her. She even heard the disciples try to dismiss her, but she stood strong! She never lost focus of her goal.

Women who can go through the testing of faith without losing hope and without feeling like Jesus has forsaken or abandoned us are the women who Jesus can rely on to tough it out in the battle to bring the Kingdom of God on earth as it is in heaven.

These are the women who can expect Jesus to say, "You have great faith! Your request is granted!" These are the women who will enjoy the fruits of fighting tooth and nail for the lives they believed were possible for them. These are women who live authentically free.

Meditation Thought
"A strong woman has faith that she is strong enough for the journey and faith that it is in the journey that she will be made strong!"—Author Unknown

Affirmation Statement
I am a woman equipped to face and overcome every challenge I encounter on my journey of faith!

Prayer
Dear Lord, my prayer this week is that you will help me develop a tough skin with a tender heart. Help me to be both wise and gentle.

Journal Reflections

_____

_____

_____

_____

_____

Week 4

Shiphrah and Puah

Reject and Resist an Oppressive Self-Image

Exodus 1

Scripture Focus

The king of Egypt said to the Hebrew midwives, whose names were Shiphrah and Puah, "When you are helping the Hebrew women during childbirth, on the delivery stool, if you see that the baby is a boy, kill him; but if it is a girl, let her live." The midwives, however, feared God and did not do what the king of Egypt had told them to do; they let the boys live. Then the king of Egypt summoned the midwives and asked them, "Why have you done this? Why have you let the boys live?" The midwives answered Pharaoh, "Hebrew women are not like Egyptian women; they are vigorous and give birth before the midwives arrive." So God was kind to the midwives and the people increased and became even more numerous. And because the midwives feared God, he gave them families of their own. Then Pharaoh gave this order to all his people: "Every boy that is born you must throw into the Nile, but let every girl live." (Exod. 1:15–22, NIV)

Reflection

Shiphrah and Puah are two women who are to be hailed as role models of true sisterhood! If you look up the phrase, "solidarity in sisterhood," you may just see the names Shiphrah and Puah. These are sisters who will have your back. These are sisters you want on your team. These are sisters with integrity, skill, wisdom, and faith. They possess the qualities that rank them high not only on the preferred list of sister friends to covet, but they rank high on God's preferred list of women to use!

God used these Hebrew women to pave the way for liberation by ensuring Hebrew boys, like Moses, didn't die at birth. God was able to use these women because they refused, rejected, and resisted the negative image their oppressive system had of them.

Pharaoh saw these midwives as women with low morals, no values, and no integrity, which is why he came to these women with an insidious plan to kill their sisters' children. With a shady view of these women, Pharaoh believed these women would partner with him to destroy and devastate their own people. And while it is true that we have seen examples of sisters stabbing one another in the back to get ahead, and while we are fully aware that because there are limited seats at the "table" for women, some will only look out for themselves, this is not the case with these Hebrew midwives.

These weren't the reality-TV-star kind of women who so often sell their dignity and integrity for a paycheck. These Hebrew women weren't for hire. They weren't for sale. They resisted the perks of the king and refused to play a role in the oppression of their own people. They rejected the idea of having a hand in inflicting pain on their sisters. These women were able to resist in this way because they didn't have the negative image of self that their oppressor had of them. They were able to reject, resist, and refuse Pharaoh's plan because they saw themselves through a different lens than Pharaoh saw them.

Shiphrah and Puah saw themselves as God-fearing protectors of the sisterhood. They couldn't fathom doing their sisters harm. They were too self-aware, too wise, and had enough reverence for God and God's creation to be complicit in a plan that would cause them to act beneath who they were created to be! At their very core and essence, they knew who they were. They hadn't taken on the oppressive image Pharaoh had of them. They didn't have an oppressive view of themselves, which made them unable to do what they had been told to do.

It was a huge risk, but they defied the king and refused to do the dirty work of an oppressive system. If we could get more women to act in the same way Shiprah and Puah did, we could build a strong sisterhood where women look out for and protect one another and where all women can thrive.

These women show us what it looks like to reject and resist an oppressive view of self, and they also show us what it looks like to live out the greatest commandment to love your neighbor as you love yourself.

Women who have a healthy view of self are least likely to inflict harm on others! Women who are committed to true solidarity in sisterhood are women who are creating a safer and more just world for women and girls.

Meditation Thought

"When they go low, we go high."—Michelle Obama

Affirmation Statement

I will make a conscious effort to never see myself through the lens of those who don't value me. I will be mindful of my worth, even when others aren't.

Prayer

Dear Lord, this week help me identify areas where I don't see myself through the lens of your loving eyes. Help me to not embrace any view of myself that doesn't reflect how fearfully and wonderfully you've created me. Help me to also be mindful to not see my sisters as less valuable than myself.

Journal Reflections

Week 5

Mahlah, Noah, Hoglah, Milkah, and Tirzah

Game Changers

Numbers 26:52-27:11

Scripture Focus

The daughters of Zelophehad son of Hepher, son of Gilead, the son of Makir, the son of Manasseh, belonged to the clans of Manasseh son of Joseph. The names of the daughters were Mahlah, Noah, Hoglah, Milkah, and Tirzah. They came forward and stood before Moses, Eleazar the priest, the leaders and the whole assembly at the entrance to the tent of meetings and said, "Our father died in the wilderness. He was not among Korah's followers, who banded together against the Lord, but he died for his own sin and left no sons. Why should our father's name disappear from his clan because he had no son? Give us property among our father's relatives." So Moses brought their case before the Lord, and the Lord said to him, "What Zelophehad's daughters are saying is right. You must certainly give them property as an inheritance among their father's relatives and give their father's inheritance to them. Say to the Israelites, 'If a man dies and leaves no son, give his inheritance to his daughter.'" (Num. 27:1–8, NIV)

Reflection

The five daughters of Zelophehad aren't widely known, but they should be. Mahlah, Noah, Hoglah, Milkah, and Tirzah are names that women and girls should know and utter often because they were game changers.

A game changer is one who disrupts the status quo and shifts the way things are done. Multiply that by five and you will see how the daughters of Zelophehad effectively changed the game of land ownership in Israel, which made a significant difference in their lives and the lives of other women in their day.

These sisters give us a different way of seeing women in Israel as we are given a glimpse of their business acumen. Agriculture was the profession of the people of Israel, and land was big business. These women, in a time when women were excluded from owning land, had enough fortitude to negotiate a slice of this business for themselves. They were clearly on the front lines of the gender equality fight long before it became a trending hashtag.

These five sisters demanded they be given their father's land that rightfully belonged to them. They argued that gender was an inadequate and unreasonable justification for keeping them from their rightful inheritance. They made such a compelling argument that Moses took their case before God. God agreed with the sisters, and the law that prevented women from inheriting land when there was no male child was changed. These sisters not only received their land, but their bold action reversed an unfair law that negatively impacted all women in Israel. Their bold action reaches even further as they remind women today that speaking up for ourselves and demanding what's ours not only improves life for us as individuals, but it also helps to lay a foundation upon which other women can build better lives. This is why it's important for women to boldly pursue everything we believe God has for us. Building on the successes of other women is what will help all women gain access and reach heights untold.

The story of these sisters is a gift to modern women because it affirms how handling our business, demanding what's ours, and being a force for change in the world are often slices of the same pie. Mahlah, Noah, Hoglah, Milkah, and Tirzah challenged the status quo and remind us that if women are to receive everything God has for us, we have to be intentional about showing up and speaking up for our own interests.

Women who fight for the promises God intended for their lives are the women who are destined to live authentically and abundantly free. Women who stake claim on what God says we can have are inherent game changers.

Meditation Thought

"Each time a woman stands up for herself, without knowing it possibly, without claiming it, she stands up for all women."—Maya Angelou

Affirmation Statement

I will not waver through unbelief regarding the promise of God because I am persuaded that God has the power to do what God has promised (a statement based on Romans 4:20–21).

Prayer

Dear Lord, this week help me to stand firm and boldly claim all that you desire for my life. Use me to be a voice to make changes for those who may not yet have the fortitude to make needed changes for themselves.

Journal Reflections

_____
_____
_____
_____
_____
_____
_____
_____
_____
_____
_____

Week 6

Queen Vashti

Dignity Threatens Insecurity

Esther 1

Scripture Focus

Queen Vashti has done wrong, not only against the king but also against all the nobles and the peoples of all the provinces of King Xerxes. For the queen's conduct will become known to all the women, and so they will despise their husbands and say, "King Xerxes commanded Queen Vashti to be brought before him, but she would not come." This very day the Persians and Median women of the nobility who have heard about the queen's conduct will respond to all the king's nobles in the same way. There will be no end of disrespect and discord. (Esther 1:16b-18, NIV)

Reflection

Every time I read Esther 1, my first instinct is always to scream, YASSSS! This first chapter alone makes me beam with pride to share a gender with such a courageous and phenomenal woman.

Queen Vashti epitomizes a woman who not only has dignity and is self-aware, but she is also that woman who looks out for other women. Modeling the true essence of what sisterhood really means, while demonstrating a high level of self-worth and value, Vashti proves worthy of the title "queen"! Her "queendom" representation is a reminder to all women to square our shoulders, adjust our crowns, and walk as if petals of roses cushioned our every step.

But beware! I must warn women that this kind of honor always comes at a price!

The price women pay for having the nerve to exhibit self-esteem and value is an unfair tax women have been paying for centuries, especially women who aren't afraid to express dissenting views from those with power, as was the case with Queen Vashti.

While Queen Vashti was holding a banquet for the women of her kingdom, she refused her husband's command to parade herself as a showpiece before a room full of drunken men. Her refusal was threatening. The men of the kingdom feared the defiant dignity Vashti displayed would become common among women. These men were fearful. They feared a kingdom full of self-loving, self-aware women who might have ambitions beyond being showpieces, bed partners, and arm candy. These men displayed a dangerous level of insecurity. And courageous, secure women are never safe around insecure men. Convinced that queen Vashti's defiance would undermine their authority and power over women, they stripped her of the crown and banished her. But when your queen status emanates from the core essence of who you are, you can be stripped of the symbol of your queen status, but never the substance.

Queen Vashti still reigned as queen, in my opinion, even after losing her crown, because any woman courageous enough to put her worth over wealth can never be downgraded.

Like Queen Vashti, a defiant woman full of courageous dignity and self-worth will always remain a threat to the insecure people. The very presence of a woman who holds herself in high regard will always irritate those who are comfortable living low. For this reason, women of courageous dignity will remain on the hit list of those who refuse to raise their standard of living!

But don't lose heart! As our dignity and love of self takes us higher, we become that much harder to hit.

Women who chose worth over wealth and character over life's comforts are the women who are truly free. They understand that the dignity of a true queen is never for sale, and they absolutely refuse to water down their core essence because it threatens those around them!

Meditation Thought

"Dignity—the word itself—has come to mean different things to different people, as many words do. It doesn't just mean always being stiff and composed. It means a belief in oneself that one is worthy of the best. Dignity means that what I have to say is important, and I will say it when it's important for me to say it. Dignity really means that I deserve the best treatment I can receive. And that I have the responsibility to give the best treatment I can to other people."—Maya Angelou

Affirmation Statement

"The kind of beauty I want most is the hard-to-get kind that comes from within—strength, courage, and dignity."—Ruby Dee

Prayer

Lord, my prayer this week is that you continue to shape me into the woman you desire me to be. In a world that would rather I conform to its norms rather than be transformed with a renewed mind, help me discern the bold steps and risks I must take to be the fearless woman of dignity and character you created me to be.

Journal Reflections

_____

_____

_____

_____

_____

_____

_____

_____

_____

Week 7

Sheerah

Building Without Blueprints

1 Chronicles 7

Scripture Focus

The descendants of Ephraim: Shuthelah Bered his son, Tahath his son, Eleadah his son, Tahath his son, Zabad his son and Shuthelah his son. Ezer and Elead were killed by the native-born men of Gath, when they went down to seize their livestock. Their father Ephraim mourned for them many days, and his relatives came to comfort him. Then he made love to his wife again, and she became pregnant and gave birth to a son. He named him Beriah, because there had been misfortune in his family. His daughter was Sheerah, who built Lower and Upper Beth Horon as well as Uzzen Sheerah. (1 Chron. 7:20–24, NIV)

Reflection

Sheerah's name should be considered for the next female superhero because what she pulls off proves she possessed skills and abilities rarely, if ever, credited to women of her day. "Superwoman" is a tittle befitting a woman who successfully builds three cities in a time where women were thought to be capable of doing little more than bearing children. A woman who masterminds an operation that builds cities, especially during a period when women struggled to even own property, deserves an *S* on her chest.

There are little details about Sheerah's life. We don't know if she broke with all traditional roles for women; we don't know if she was married with children or not, but we do know she was an outlier. We know that in a profession that was only accredited to men, she was unlike any other woman we've ever encountered in scripture. Blazing her own trail and without having blueprints or footsteps of other women who were successful in this line of work to follow, Sheerah conceived and implemented a vision in the face of what I'm sure had to be significant obstacles.

I'm confident that as a woman, there were those who told her she couldn't build cities. I'm convinced that she faced more than her share of naysayers, haters, and those who felt she was crossing the line, overreaching, and taking on more that she could handle. These are things women hear when we attempt that which has never before been done. These are things women hear when we step outside of the boxes in which others expect us to remain. I'm convinced that Sheerah, like many women today, had to deal with negative unsupportive voices as she launched her vision.

Women always have to contend with negative voices as we share our plans to build the futures we envision for ourselves. Whether it's owning a business, holding political office, or pastoring a church, women are constantly doubted. But Sheerah is a reminder to women to go for it! She is a convincing reminder of just how capable women are.

If Sheerah could successfully build three cities—one of which she named after herself because she could—and if she could build these cities without blueprints and without having examples of other women who had similar success, surely women today can build the futures we desire.

Unlike Sheerah, women today have a long list of women from Madam C. J. Walker, to Oprah, to Shonda Rhimes, who all built million-dollar brands from scratch to encourage and inspire us. These women, much like Sheerah, took their vision and ran with it, falling and failing along the way, but persevering until the vision was built.

Sheerah gives encouragement to women who have visions to create and build. She reminds women that if you can see it in your mind's eye, you can manifest it. She reminds women that even if it has never been done before, do it anyway. Blueprints aren't necessary.

Women who use internal blueprints to build the future they desire—women who are guided by a vision within—are the women who will live most authentically! These women are the freest among us!

Meditative Thought
God will give us the gift of a vision. It's up to us to believe in it and work toward manifesting it.

Affirmation Statement
I am a trailblazer. I will not fear, hesitate, or shy away from being a first.

Prayer
Dear Lord, this week remind me that I can do all things through Christ. Help me remember to open myself up to the "new thing" you are looking to do on this earth!

Journal Reflections

_____

_____

_____

_____

_____

_____

_____

_____

_____

_____

_____

_____

_____

Week 8

Rahab

An Appropriate Response to Fear

Joshua 2

Scripture Focus

Before the spies lay down for the night, she went up on the roof and said to them, "I know that the Lord has given you this land and that a great fear of you has fallen on us, so that all who live in this country are melting in fear because of you. We have heard how the Lord dried up the water of the Red Sea for you when you came out of Egypt, and what you did to Sihon and Og, the two kings of Amorites east of the Jordan, whom you completely destroyed. When we heard of it, our hearts melted in fear and everyone's courage failed because of you, for the Lord your God is God in heaven and above and on the earth below. "Now then, please swear to me by the Lord that you will show kindness to my family, because I have sown kindness to you. Give me a sure sign that you will spare the lives of my father and mother, my brothers and sisters, and all who belong to them, and that you will save us from death." "Our lives for your lives!" the men assured her.

"If you don't tell what we are doing, we will treat you kindly and faithfully when the Lord gives us this land." (Josh. 2:8–14, NIV)

Reflection

There are many acronyms for the word FEAR, but my favorite is, "**Face Everything And Rise**." This is what Rahab inspires.

"Fearless" is not the most familiar term used to describe Rahab, mainly because of the way she is often presented to us. Rahab was a prostitute, and just about every passage in the Bible that mentions her (with the exception of Matthew)—Joshua, Hebrews, James—makes sure we remember this little detail about her. Her profession, however, is not what she should be most remembered for, nor is it what gained her a place in the family lineage of Jesus. What gained Rahab honorable mentions throughout scripture, what afforded her a leaf on Jesus's family tree, and what she should be most remembered for was her courage, how she responded to fear, and how her response was the catalyst to a future she could have never imagined.

Fear is something we all experience. I don't care how spiritual we are. I don't care if you, like some women I know, have a Post-it note stuck to your bathroom mirror to daily remind you, "God didn't give us the spirit of fear." We still experience it.

It's inevitable!

There are just some circumstances in life that cause our stomachs to drop, our hearts to race, and the hairs on the backs of our necks to raise! Denying fear doesn't convey our spiritual aptitude, but rather how we respond to fear. It's whether we respond to fear from a position of helplessness or hopefulness. And while we can ascribe many titles to Rahab, helpless wouldn't be one of them.

As the threat of death loomed for Rahab and the entire kingdom in which she lived, she didn't give in to a feeling of helplessness. She didn't curl up in a fetal position believing all was lost. She went to work. She weighed her options and devised a plan to save herself and her entire family, and she did this while defying the king of Jericho.

Sometimes defiance is the only appropriate response! When there was a choice to be made between joining forces with the Almighty God and remaining a resident of a kingdom that left her so few choices that prostitution became her profession, defiance was necessary! Rahab is another defiant woman of faith we are fortunate to read about. She is another woman who refused to allow the authoritative power over her to destroy her and prevent her from a life she believed was possible for her.

Rahab was a resourceful and discerning woman who didn't allow the fear to consume her, and she reminds women how to respond to fear with calculated wisdom.

Rahab first compels us to face our fears. We can't afford to stick our heads in the sand and hide from the realities of life. We have to face that which we fear. This is what true courage is. Courage is not the absence of fear. Courage is facing your fears.

Second, Rahab shows us that we must discern our fears! Rahab looked for where God was in the situation and it became her guiding star. She proves to us that when we seek God during our greatest moments of fear, and when we determine in our minds that we are going to hitch our wagons to wherever God is and wherever God is going, God will not disappoint.

Third, Rahab shows us that we must rise to actively challenge our fears. So often we are told to just pray about troubling matters, but Rahab understood that action was required. This maybe why James 2:25 references Rahab when he says, "Faith without works is dead." It was Rahab's action in the face of fear that led her to a new life.

Rahab reminds women that life will constantly present us reasons to fear, but she also reminds us that we can chose a helpless or a hopeful response to that fear. Women who chose a hopeful response are women who believe and sense that God has more for us. These are the women who believe the evidence of things unseen.

God has a place of promise for all God's women, but often that place of promise is on the other side of a fear we must face!

Meditation Thought
You must do the thing you fear you cannot do.

Affirmation Statement
"I will never be afraid to trust my unknown future to a known God!"—Corrie Ten Boom

Prayer
Dear Lord, this week help me to always have an appropriate response to fear. Remind me that fears are an attempt to keep me complacent and away from my intended places of promise. In the midst of my deepest fears, remind me that I am more than a conqueror and that the experience of fear is also an opportunity to exercise my faith.

Journal Reflections

The Woman Who Washed Jesus's Feet

An Audience of One

Luke 7

Scripture Focus

When one of the Pharisees invited Jesus to have dinner with him, he went to the Pharisee's house and reclined at the table. A woman in that town who lived a sinful life learned that Jesus was eating at the Pharisee's house, so she came there with an alabaster jar of perfume. As she stood behind him at his feet weeping, she began to wet his feet with her tears. Then she wiped them with her hair, kissed them and poured perfume on them. When the Pharisee who had invited him saw this, he said to himself, "If this man were a prophet, he would know who is touching him and what kind of woman she is—that she is a sinner." Jesus answered him, "Simon, I have something to tell you." "Tell me, teacher," he said. "Two people owed money to a certain moneylender. One owed him five hundred denarii, and the other fifty. Neither of them had the money to pay him back, so he forgave the debts of both. Now which of them will love him more?" Simone replied, "I suppose the one who had the bigger debt forgiven." "You have judged correctly," Jesus said. Then he turned to the woman and said to Simon, "Do you see this woman? I came into your house. You did not give me any water for my feet, but she wet my feet with her tears and wiped them with her hair. You did not give me a kiss, but this woman, from the time I entered, has not stopped kissing my feet. You did not put oil on my head, but she has poured perfume on my feet. Therefore, I tell you, her many sins have ben forgiven—as her great love has shown. But whoever has been forgiven little loves little." Then Jesus said to her, "Your sins are forgiven." The other guests began to say among themselves, "Who is this who even forgives sins?" Jesus said to the woman, "Your faith has saved you; go in peace." (Luke 7:36–50, NIV)

Reflection

The story of the woman who washes Jesus's feet is one of the clearest pictures of a defiant woman of faith. The act of worship she displayed is not only insight into the depth of gratitude and love she had for Jesus, but it is also a defiant act of rebellion against those who saw her as shamefully unworthy. Her courageous act of worship and her bold rebellion are both pointedly instructive for contemporary women seeking to live in an abundance of freedom. They remind women that true freedom requires both liberation from the prison of our past mistakes and the prison of other people's opinions about our past mistakes.

Nothing paralyzes us more on our journey to live authentically and abundantly free than being chained to the mistakes of the past and allowing other people to hold us captive to that past. In one act of worship, this woman broke free of both.

This woman's reputation of "sinning" was widely known. She had the kind of reputation that made her least likely to secure an invite to dinner parties such as the one mentioned. Yet fully aware that her presence was not welcomed and fully aware of the disapproving stares and whispers she might receive, she showed up to the dinner anyway.

Such bold behavior had to have stemmed from a previous encounter with Jesus where he made her feel whole and complete; where he made her feel like her past, no matter how dark, didn't matter. Only a real faith encounter with Jesus can strengthen us to a magnitude where we show up in places with our heads held high, dignity intact, and unbothered by those who refuse to see our worth and value.

This woman didn't allow her mistakes to define or diminish her; neither did she allow those who knew her past cause her to live her life in hiding and in shame. As she refuses to live in the shadows and refuses to be shacked by the opinions others have of her, she encourages contemporary women to do the same. She reminds those of us who've had some less-than-shining moments to fully embrace ourselves, flaws and all, and live out loud, even in the presence of those who believe we are wrong and unworthy to do so.

The dinner host saw this woman as shameful and believed her past disqualified her from being in the very presence of the honored guest, but Jesus, the honored guest, reverses the shame. He spotlights the host's shameful behavior and highlights the woman's action. Jesus sees her action as honorable, while the host's action, or lack thereof, is seen as dishonorable.

This reversal Jesus does is a reminder to women to always live our lives for an audience of One. It is a reminder that when we live our lives for the approval of Jesus alone, not caring about the response and reaction we get from people, it is the epitome of living in authentic and true freedom.

The woman who washed Jesus's feet refused to live in the prison of other people's opinions and refused to allow the mistakes of her past to lock her out of the future that was still open to her.

Women who have made mistakes, large and small, but who refuse to allow those mistakes to imprison us are a valuable witness and asset to the Kingdom. These women prove what a merciful God we serve, and they make the case that all have sinned and fallen short yet all are still valuable and welcome!

Mediation Thought

One of the most defining moments in life is realizing that our mistakes don't nullify our worth. We have intrinsic value.

Affirmation Statement

I am imperfect and worthy of love at the same time!

Prayer

Dear Lord, help me remember that shame is the painful feeling that we are unworthy of love. Remind me of your unwavering love for me, especially in moments I've disappointed myself and fallen short of your expectations. Help me to always remember that no matter what I've done, I'm loved!

Journal Reflections

_____
_____
_____
_____
_____
_____
_____
_____
_____
_____
_____
_____
_____
_____
_____
_____
_____
_____
_____
_____

Week 10

Huldah

2 Kings 22:14-20

Focus Scripture

Hilkiah the priest, Ahikam, Akbor, Shaphan and Asaiah went to speak to the prophet Huldah, who was the wife of Shallum son of Tikvah, the son of Harhas, Keeper of the wardrobe. She lived in Jerusalem, in the New Quarter. She said to them, "This is what the Lord, the God of Israel, says: Tell the man who sent you to me..." (2 Kings 22:14–15, NIV)

Reflection

H uldah is another woman of scripture who flies under the radar of significant biblical figures, but who lands squarely on our list of powerful and inspiring women. As it is with many women in the Bible, to uncover her greatness and see the rich contributions she made, it requires us to read between the lines of her story.

Huldah was one of the rare female prophets. Her profession in and of itself is one where she had to defy the more traditional roles for women of her day.

As a prophet she was respected as one who communicated with God. God spoke to her and she spoke to God. She was so well respected in her uncommon role that those in authority, the king of Israel and the priest, sought after her. They sought after her even as the prophet Jeremiah, who is more widely known to us, was active during this time.

To be sought after in this way and especially during this particular period, Huldah had to be a woman with an impeccable reputation. In a field dominated by men, she had to be exceptional. She had to be at the top of her game. She had to be a trusted voice that provided wise counsel. She also had to lead a respectable life in order to be the sought after prophet she was because women, then and now, are always held to a higher standard than our male counterparts.

Whether it's in the corporate world, the church, or social groups, women have to perform exceptionally well and have impeccable reputations to even be considered for certain positions, especially those traditionally held by men. Women often have to not only meet, but exceed the qualifications to acquire positions in male-dominated fields. Our ability to exceed is also what makes us sought-after women.

It's no surprise that Hulda excelled in her role as prophet to the point that the king and the priest came looking for her and her counsel. She was skilled, gifted, and more importantly, created for the position she held. When we witness women excelling in any field, dominated by men or not, it is evident that they connected an innate gift to their life's work; because God is the giver of all gifts, this connection is Divine.

Reading between the lines of Huldah's story reminds us that the fruits of her exceptional work and reputation were the results of her relationship and connection with the Divine. Her life wasn't compartmentalized. Her job and activity with God weren't separate things. Her work was fueled and informed by her relationship and connection with God. There was synergy between what she did in life as work and who she was. This combination is what makes us successful and sought after.

In a world where men still dominate, it's important for women to pursue positions and have representation in every field. Huldah is a reminder that women can be just as successful in fields that are dominated by men.

Women, like Huldah, who have an intimate, Divine connection, who work hard at perfecting the gifts and skills entrusted to them, and who connect their God-given purpose with their life's work are often the women who are the most satisfied, fulfilled, and sought after.

Meditation Thought

A woman who takes as much time to cultivate the interior as she does her exterior will be a woman who is sought by many.

Affirmation Statement

I am a woman of substance and skill. When I'm connected to my Divine calling, the sky is the limit.

Prayer

Dear Lord, this week continue to confirm the purpose for my life and help me to fearlessly carry out that purpose with integrity, grace, and love.

Journal Reflections

_____

_____

_____

_____

_____

_____

_____

_____

_____

_____

_____

_____

_____

_____

_____

Week 11

Sarai (Sarah)

Don't Be a Best-Kept Secret

Genesis 12:10-20

Scripture Focus

As he (Abram) was about to enter Egypt, he said to his wife Sarai, "I know what a beautiful woman you are. When the Egyptians see you, they will say, 'This is his wife.' Then they will kill me but will let you live. Say you are my sister, so that I will be treated well for your sake and my life will be spared because of you." When Abram came to Egypt, the Egyptians saw that Sarai was a very beautiful woman. And when Pharaoh's officials saw her, they praised her to Pharaoh, and she was taken into his palace. He treated Abram well for her sake, and Abram acquired sheep and cattle, male and female donkeys, male and female servants, and camels. (Gen. 12:11–16, NIV)

Reflection

Sarah, the woman who inspired hope and reminded women just how faithful God is when she became a mother in the latter season of life, also gives women another important reminder. A scene from Sarah's life, before her name was changed from Sarai, reminds women just how dangerous it is to be kept a secret by a man who is supposed to love you. As Malcolm X reminds us that black women are the most unprotected, neglected, and disrespected women in America, this is a heads-up that needs to be heeded.

This behind-the-scenes look at Sarai's and Abram's relationship mirrors contemporary relationships where men convince women that it's best for all parties involved if the relationship is kept a secret. Abram, like most men who are looking to have their cake and eat it too, made a convincing argument to Sarai as to why she should keep their relationship a secret. He appealed to her protective, nurturing side. Abram used the same language manipulating men have been using on women for centuries. He makes it appear that the secrecy of the relationship was protection for "them" when it was actually protection for him.

Under the cover of "secret relationships," men benefit while women are exposed to hurt and harm. Abram received cattle and servants because of the secrecy, while Sarai was taken, against her will, to be the wife of Pharaoh. Secret relationships often provide men the freedom and cover to receive extra benefits outside the relationship while women's hearts are left exposed to hurt and harm.

Sarai's story is a red flag for modern women seeking loving and nurturing relationships. Her story reminds women that when a man is willing to risk your well-being or willing to risk sharing you with another, as was the case with Abram, he doesn't value you. When a man choses to keep a significant relationship a secret, it is a red flag that he doesn't see true value in the woman, nor does he see her as the gift God intended women to be.

From God's response in this story, it's clear that God didn't approve of Abram keeping his and Sarai's relationship a secret. Well-kept secrets of this kind do more harm than good.

Women who reject being the secret lovers of those who really want to have their cake and eat it too are women who make themselves available for unconditional love with those who are capable of expressing love openly and freely.

Meditation Thought

There is a difference between privacy and secrecy. Your relationship can be private without you being a secret.

Affirmation Statement

I am too wonderful, too beautiful, and too bright a star to be kept in darkness.

Prayer

Dear Lord, this week give me the strength to walk away from anyone who only choses to love me behind closed doors. Help me to remember that nothing real can grow and flourish in darkness.

Journal Reflections

_____
_____
_____
_____
_____
_____
_____
_____
_____
_____
_____
_____
_____
_____
_____
_____
_____
_____
_____
_____
_____

Week 12

Queen of Sheba

In Pursuit of a Rich Life

1 Kings

Scripture Focus

When the queen of Sheba heard about the fame of Solomon and his relationship to the Lord, she came to test Solomon with hard questions. Arriving at Jerusalem with a very great caravan—with camels carrying spices, large quantities of gold, and precious stones—she came to Solomon and talked with him about all that she had on her mind. Solomon answered all her questions; nothing was too hard for the king to explain to her. When the queen of Sheba saw all the wisdom of Solomon and the palace he had built, the food on his table, the seating of his officials, the attending servants in their robes, his cupbearers, and the burnt offerings he made at the temple of the Lord, she was overwhelmed. She said to the king, "The report I heard in my own country about your achievements and your wisdom is true. But I did not believe these things until I came and saw with my own eyes. Indeed, not even half was told me; in wisdom and wealth you have far exceeded the report I heard. How happy your people must be! How happy your officials, who continually stand before you and hear your wisdom! Praise be to the Lord Your God, who has delighted in you and placed you on the throne of Israel. Because of the Lord's eternal love for Israel, he is made you king to maintain justice and righteousness." (1 Kings 10:1–13, NIV)

Reflection

The queen of Sheba, simply put, is a woman I admire. I admire powerful women who have substance and are tastefully balanced. I admire women who have reached the pinnacle of success by amassing power, position, authority, and wealth, but who still thirst for wisdom, truth, and the Divine. In these few verses about the queen of Sheba, she is painted as such a woman.

The queen of Sheba is a woman who possessed great wealth and who sat at the head seat of a powerful kingdom, but who must have also sensed that something was missing. I imagine the things she acquired were somewhat unfulfilling outside of a deeper relationship and connection with the Creator. Wealth and power are never really enough to satisfy a woman of substance. A woman of substance and balance needs, along with financial security and fulfilling work, a life-changing, enriching, and meaningful relationship to be truly satisfied and completely fulfilled; this is what draws the queen of Sheba to Jerusalem.

The queen of Sheba didn't go to Jerusalem with her impressive caravan because she was interested in a personal relationship with King Solomon. The opening passage makes it clear that her interest was in his relationship with the Lord. She heard about King Solomon's fame, but she came with an interest in the One behind the fame.

Yes, it's true. She was impressed with Solomon and overwhelmed at the sight of his kingdom, but she didn't credit Solomon as the source. She credited the God of Solomon. She said, "Praise be to the Lord Your God, who has delighted in you and placed you on the throne of Israel. Because of the Lord's eternal love for Israel, he has made you king."

In a time when kingdoms and monarchies aligned forces through marriages to increase and/or strengthen power, this queen gives no intimation that this is her desire. The queen of Sheba is another woman who forces us to see women in scripture through a more empowered lens.

The poise this queen displays gives us a glimpse into the security and self-assurance with which she reigned. It's how all of us modern queens of this contemporary age should reign. The glamour and majesty of Solomon's kingdom didn't cause her to lose focus. His power and authority didn't cloud her ability to see clearly. In fact, she proves herself to be a woman of great clarity when she attributes who Solomon is and what he has to his relationship with God! She wasn't as interested in the man as she was in the God inside the man.

The queen of Sheba reminds women that it is a relationship with God that is the foundation of a rich life. She reminds us that if we pursue God with everything we have, it may not result in an abundance of financial wealth, but we will experience the riches of the abundant life God intended for us.

It is both dangerous and disappointing to reduce a rich and fulfilling life to power and wealth. The queen of Sheba had both, and yet she was still in search of something richer and more meaningful.

Women who pursue God because God is the source and the strength of our lives, and not merely a resource, are women who are destined to live rich, full, and free.

Meditation Thought

There is no amount of silver and gold in the entire world that can make you feel as rich and satisfied as a relationship with God!

Affirmation Statement

I am already a priceless treasure, and the only thing I seek that can add more value to me is a richer connection with God.

Prayer

Dear Lord, this week help me to remember that pursing your heart will expose me to a far richer life than pursing what's in your hand. Help me to remember that what you provide for me is secondary to who you are to me.

Journal Reflections

_____

_____

_____

_____

_____

_____

_____

_____

_____

_____

_____

_____

_____

_____

_____

_____

_____

_____

_____

_____

_____

_____

_____

_____

_____

_____

_____

_____

Woman with the Spirit

A Little Is Just Enough

Act 16

Scripture Focus

Once when we were going to the place of prayer, we were met by a female slave who had a spirit by which she predicted the future. She earned a great deal of money for her owners by fortune-telling. She followed Paul and the rest of us, shouting, "These men are servants of the Most High God, who are telling you the way to be saved." She kept this up for many days. Finally Paul became so annoyed that he turned around and said to the spirit, "In the name of Jesus Christ I command you to come out of her!" At that moment the spirit left her. (Acts 16:16–18, NIV)

Reflection

The woman with the spirit is another reminder of why it's important for con-temporary women to see women in the Bible through a fresh and empower-ing lens.

If we look beyond the fact that this woman had spirit or was possessed, we will not only see ourselves, but we will be reminded of a very important lesson. The lesson she reminds us is that we don't need to be perfect, live flawlessly, or have it all together in order to live free. Her story reminds us that if we have just a little of the right thing together, it's enough to put us on a path to complete liberation.

A deeper look at this woman reveals she is a walking, talking paradox. She is complex. She has layers. She, like most women I know, is "complicated." It's true. She has a spirit that causes her to behave in ways that aren't "of God," but I find this to be true of all of us! All of us, under the influence of a spirit other than the Holy Spirit, have done things that have caused us to ask ourselves, "What possessed me to do that?" But where this woman begins to resemble most women I know is when she begins to articulate some sacred truth.

This woman, who is being ungodly influenced, is also able to recognize, discern, and articulate the Divine. She knows and can see and sense God's presence. She makes this clear when she sees Paul and those with him and says, "These men are servants of the Most High God, who are telling you the way to be saved." It is when she discloses this sacred truth that I was able to not only see our similarities, but see how having just a little of the right thing—the ability to recognize the Divine—is enough to free us! With just a glimpse of God's presence as Paul passed her by, she saw and sensed an opportunity for freedom. But that freedom wouldn't come without a fight.

Paul ignored this woman for many days, which is not uncommon for women who struggle in the fight for liberation. Women who clamor for freedom are often ignored, tuned out, or invisible. But she is a reminder to women to never quit. In every place where women go unheard and unseen or are in one form of chains or another, we have to be as relentlessly vocal about our freedom as this woman.

Her determination is another example of how women must fight tooth and nail to freely live our lives.

I refuse to see this woman as just some demonically possessed woman. I see her as a woman who demanded the freedom that she knew deep inside belonged to her. I see her as a woman who took full advantage of the mustard seed of hope that was ignited in her when she encountered the Divine. Her story should remind and encourage every woman that a glimpse of the truth of who God is and a relentless acknowledgement of that truth is all that is required to began a journey down the path to abundant freedom.

Women who may not have all their ducks in a row, but who understand that a little faith in God goes a long way, are women who are destined to live free.

Mediation Thought
Just a little of God is enough to change your entire existence.

Affirmation Statement
I am perfectly imperfect! I am fully loved by God! I am worthy and deserving of living in total freedom.

Prayer
Dear Lord, this week remind me that I don't need to have everything together in life to live abundantly free.

Journal Reflections

_____

_____

_____

_____

_____

_____

_____

_____

_____

_____

_____

_____

_____

_____

_____

_____

Week 14

Orpah

Never Regret Choosing Yourself

Ruth 1:1-14

Scripture Focus

Then Naomi said to her two daughters-in-law, "Go back, each of you, to your mother's home. May the Lord show you kindness, as you have shown kindness to your dead husbands and to me. May the Lord grant that each of you will find security, each of you in the home of anther husband." Then she kissed them goodbye and they wept aloud and said to her, "We will go back with you to your people." But Naomi said, "Return home, my daughters. Why would you come with me? Am I going to have any more sons who could become your husbands? Return home, my daughters; I am too old to have another husband. Even if I thought there was still hope for me—even if I had a husband tonight and then gave birth to sons—would you wait until they grew up? Would you remain unmarried for them? No, my daughters. It is more bitter for me than you, because the Lord's hand has turned against me!" At this they wept aloud again. Then Orpah kissed her mother-in-law goodbye, but Ruth clung to her. (Ruth 1:6–14, NIV)

Reflection

Orpah should be esteemed and held in honor for being a woman who understands the necessity of putting yourself first. Too often women embrace a subconscious belief that it's appropriate to put the needs of others before our own. The nurturing instinct in women can too often cause us to prioritize ourselves to the bottom of the list in our own lives, but not Orpah.

Orpah stands as a model for women who give themselves permission to make choices that suit their needs, wants, and desires. Her short story is a reminder to women that if we don't make choices for ourselves, we may end up in a foreign and distant place away from the life we were intended to live.

Orpah was presented with a choice. And after some careful thought and deliberation, she made a different decision from her sister-in-law, Ruth. She made a decision that considered what she wanted and what was best for her.

When Orpah's mother-in-law painted in grim detail what the reality would be for a chance at a new family, it resonated with Orpah. She considered her chances for marriage and children in a land where Moabite women weren't the first choice. She probably considered that she more than likely wouldn't have suitors lined up at the door. With this in mind, she kissed her mother-in-law and went along her way.

Applause! Applause! Applause to women who are comfortable and perfectly fine making decisions that lead to their abundant lives. Applause to women who reject the guilt often associated with putting yourself first.

Whether we are like Orpah, who seemingly made a decision based on her desire for a family, or whether we are making decisions based on a desire to climb the corporate ladder, ether way, the choice is ours to make. These choices are too important to hand over to others or even to allow outside voices to significantly influence our decisions.

It was both refreshing and inspiring to see how Orpah didn't allow herself to be swayed by Ruth's decision to stay. Who knows whether Ruth decided to go forward with her mother-in-law because she had nothing to go back to, whereas Orpah could have had a welcoming family waiting to embrace her.

In subtle ways, Orpah is presented as having made the wrong decision because here it seems to imply a rejection of God. I don't see it that way. I see Orpah as a woman using her God-given sensibilities to make the best decision for her life. I personally believe God smiled with pride as Orpah decided to journey a path she felt was the best path for her.

Women who make their own choices are happier, more satisfied, and more fulfilled. They understand that being able to make your own choices is true freedom.

Meditation Thought

Prioritizing ourselves to the top of our lists is not selfish; it's self-care, and it's the best choice we can make for ourselves.

Affirmation Statement

I am responsible for my own happiness; therefore I will not regret making choices that bring joy and peace to my life.

Prayer

Dear Lord, this week help me be mindful that the only way I can experience the abundant life you afforded me is to take exceptional care of myself and to make decisions that direct me to live my best life.

Journal Reflections

_____
_____
_____
_____
_____
_____
_____
_____
_____
_____
_____
_____
_____
_____

Jephthah's Daughter

I'm Not Your Sacrifice

Judges 11:30-39

Scripture Focus

And Jephthah made a vow to the Lord: If you give me the Ammonites into my hands, whatever comes out of the door of my house to meet me when I return in triumph from the Ammonites will be the Lord's, and I will sacrifice it as a burnt offering. (*Judg. 11:30–31, NIV*)

When Jephthah returned to his home in Mizpah, who should come out to meet him but his daughter, dancing to the sound of timbrels! She was an only child. Except for her he had neither son nor daughter. When he saw her, he tore his clothes and cried, "Oh no, my daughter! You have brought me down and I am devastated. I have made a vow to the Lord that I can not break." "My father," she replied, "You have given your word to the Lord. Do to me just as you promised..." (*Judg. 11:34–36, NIV*)

Reflection

This cautionary tale of Jephthah's daughter is a warning for women to never become the sacrifice in someone else's misguided devotion to God. This young woman's story is a reminder to be careful in allowing ourselves to be offered up as the scapegoats in a sacrifice God never required.

In our desire to be good disciples, it's easy to want to help people honor their commitments to God. But when helping them hurts us and causes us to suffer, we have to draw the line.

Without questioning, Jephthah's daughter agreed to her father's misguided devotion to God. Had she asked a few questions, she might have determined that God never asked her father for a sacrifice, nor did God agree to the offer he extended. She might have discovered that making a "if you do this for me, I'll do this for you" pact rarely, if ever, works with God. Had she questioned, perhaps she would have discovered that based on Deuteronomy 12:31, God was abhorrently against child sacrifices, which would have made her sacrifice displeasing and unacceptable.

Her story is a painful reminder of just how imperative it is to not be a blind follower of people. Jephthah's daughter cautions us to remember that it is perfectly fine to question family, religious, and political authority as well as anyone who would have us believe our suffering is a righteous or justifiable act before God. Questioning directives to be self-sacrificing is critical, even when it comes from those who love us and claim to have our best interests at heart, like it was in this story. Sometimes people mean well, but their attempts to be faithful to God can still be misguided. In addition, we have to also be careful as a desire to be loyal servants to God can compel us, like it did this young girl, to carry burdens God never intended.

Women who understand that God would never require us to emotionally, mentally, physically, or morally sacrifice ourselves as an act of devotion are women who are less likely to be distracted and led astray on their journey to living the free abundant life Jesus offers.

Meditation Thought

God says, "For I desire steadfast love and not sacrifice, the knowledge of God rather than burnt offerings."—Hosea 6:6, NRSV

Affirmation Statement

I will question spiritual, political, social, and moral directives that require me to be harmed or that don't have my best interests at heart.

Prayer

Dear Lord, this week help me to remember that the sacrifice that you desire most is a humble spirit and a repented heart. Help me to always remember that you have not called me to be the human sacrifice of another; the sacrifice you gave on Calvary was sufficient.

Journal Reflections

_____

_____

_____

_____

_____

_____

_____

_____

_____

_____

_____

_____

_____

_____

_____

_____

_____

_____

_____

_____

_____

_____

Week 16

Moses's Sister

Their Eyes Are Watching Us

Exodus 2

Scripture Focus

Now a man of the house of Levi married a Levite woman, and she became pregnant and gave birth to a son. When she saw that he was a fine child, she hid him for three months. But when she could hide him no longer, she got a papyrus basket for him and coated it with tar and pitch. Then she placed the child in it and put in among the reeds along the bank of the Nile. His sister stood at a distance to see what would happen to him. Then Pharaoh's daughter went down to the Nile to bathe, and her attendants were walking along the river bank. She saw the basket among the reeds and sent her female slave to get it. She opened it and saw the baby. He was crying, and she felt sorry for him. "This is one of the Hebrew babies," she said. Then his sister asked Pharaoh's daughter, "Shall I go and get one of the Hebrew women to nurse the baby for you?" "Yes, go," she answered. So the girl went and got the baby's mother. Pharaoh's daughter sad to her, "Take this baby and nurse him for me, and I will pay you." So the woman took the baby and nursed him. When the child grew older, she took him

50

to Pharaoh's daughter and he became her son. She named him Moses, saying, "I drew him out of the water." (Exod. 2:1–10, NIV)

Reflection

I am a woman who takes great pride in the responsibility I have in mentoring, empowering, and protecting young women and girls in the generation behind me. In working with girls, I'm mindful that the impact I will have on them has more to do with what I show them than what I tell them. The old adage that says, "do what I say and not what I do" has proven to be the least effective in influencing young people. It didn't work on me. I suppose it won't work on them.

How we live has more influence on the next generation than what we say. Actions speak louder than words; they have more impact, and young people are more likely to mimic what we do over what we say. Moses's sister is a model of how true this is.

This young girl watches and gleans form her mother and then implements what she witnessed and learned.

Moses's sister, at the time of this passage, is said to be between the ages of seven and twelve years old. And like all girls her age, she watched and learned valuable lessons from her mother. We know she had this watchful eye on her mother because she was there watching from a distance as her mother put Moses in the Nile. But it's clear she was watching long before that.

I imagine the girl watched her mother figure out how to save her son in a system of oppression that wanted to kill him. I imagine this young girl watching and learning from her mother what it means to defy and resist hateful regimes that see no value in your people. I imagine she watched her mother as she hid Moses for three months. I imagine she watched as her mother agonized over putting Moses in the Nile. I imagine she watched as her mother's radical faith overrode her rational fear of floating her son down a dangerous river.

All the watching this young girl did was not lost on her. It becomes evident that she picked up some valuable skills of how to outwit your oppressors. Moses's mother's action modeled and produced an intuitive skill in this young girl that prepared her to be used by God in God's ultimate plan for the liberation of the people of Israel.

When her brother ended up in the unlikely place of the Pharaoh's daughter's arms, this young girl sprang into action, brokering a deal that would not only heal and relieve her mother's heart, but get her mother paid at the same time.

Where does a girl seven to twelve years old get such skill that could produce such an outcome? She gets it from her mother!

What we do as women will certainly impact the next generation of women. And if we want to have a strong, powerful generation of women who will continue to break down the glass ceilings and provide more seating at the table, we have to make sure we are showing young women how to fight in a world where they are seen as less than others.

We have to question what young girls glean from our lives. What are we showing young, impressionable girls about the kind of women they should aspire to be? Answering these questions will ensure that generations of women to come are always prepared for the fight before them.

Women who leave a strong and positive legacy behind them are not only making their mark on this world, but they are blazing a trail for others to follow that will have impact for generations to come!

Mediation Thought

"What you do speaks so loudly that I cannot hear what you say."—Ralph Waldo Emerson

Affirmation Statement

I will forever be mindful of how I live because the decisions I make will show up in my children, my community, and in the world.

Prayer

Dear Lord, this week help me to be mindful of those you've placed in my sphere of influence. Help me to remember the greater impact I can have on this world by being a positive image that helps to shape the next generation.

Journal Reflections

Hagar

The Struggle Is Real

Genesis 16

Scripture Focus

Now Sarai, Abram's wife, had borne him no children. But she had an Egyptian slave named Hagar, so she said to Abram, "The Lord has kept me from having children. Go, sleep with my slave; perhaps I can build a family through her." Abram Agreed to what Sarai said. So after Abram had been living in Canaan ten years, Sarai his wife took her Egyptian slave Hagar and gave her to her husband to be his wife. He slept with Hagar, and she conceived. When she knew she was pregnant, she began to despise her mistress. Then Sarai said to Abram, "You are responsible for the wrong I am suffering. I put my slave in your arms, and now that she knows she is pregnant, she despises me. May the Lord judge between you and me." "Your slave is in your hands," Abram said. "Do with her whatever you think best." Then Sarai mistreated Hagar; so she fled from her. The angel of the Lord found Hagar near a spring in the desert; it was the spring that is beside the road to Shur. And he said, "Hagar, slave of Sarai, where have you come from, and where are you going?" "I'm running away from my mistress Sarai," she answered. Then the angel of the Lord told her, "Go back to your mistress and submit to her." The angel added, "I will increase your descendants so much that they will be too numerous to count." The angel of the Lord also said to her: "You are now with child and you will have a son. You shall name him Ishmael, for the Lord has heard your misery. He will be a wild donkey of a man; his hand will be against everyone and everyone's hand against him, and he will live in hostility toward all his brothers." She gave this name to the Lord who spoke to her: "You are the God who sees me," for she said, "I have now seen the One who sees me." (Gen. 16:1–13, NIV)

Reflection

There comes a time in every woman's life where we question God. Even those of us with the strongest of faith have to admit that we've been to this place of uncertainty with God. We've questioned if God loves us, if God is paying attention to what's happening with us, and sometimes, if we are honest, we've questioned if there is a God at all. We tend to ask these questions when we are going through some of the most unimaginable pain and disappointment.

When we read Hagar's story, these questions can't help but come to mind. She is a slave who has no control over her life, body, or her future. She is misused and mistreated; ironically, when she flees because she's had enough, God not only finds her and questions her, but God instructs her to go back and submit herself to the conditions she fled.

What, God? Why, God?

These are the questions that immediately come to mind when reading Hagar's story. These are the questions that we ask, not only of Hagar's story, but of our own stories when we can't make sense of the pain, suffering, and disappointment we experience. How do we reconcile our trust in God in these moments?

I don't have a magical answer—and don't believe anyone who tries to sell you one. The truth is, we must wrestle with our faith!

Wresting, doubting, and struggling in faith are not ungodly. These are real factors in a relationship between an Infinite God and a finite creation. God is not afraid of, nor does God punish us, for struggling, questioning, and wrestling with our faith.

Sometimes the wrestling yields answers and sometimes it doesn't, unfortunately. Sometimes we have to accept that life is a mystery that we won't understand. Sometimes we resolve that God allows us to go through tough experiences because God is preparing and strengthening us. And sometimes, like in the case of Hagar, God has a plan and a reward on the other side of the pain we experience.

There are times when God is silent in our lives. There are times when bad things happen and there are no explanations given. These are the times we have to allow our faith in a God who promises peace that surpasses understanding, but who does not necessarily answer, to win the wrestling match.

This is grown-woman faith, and it's not for the faint at heart!

We don't always receive answers to life's most difficult and most painful questions, but we can have a peace and assurance that God is with us in every difficult circumstance. Just as Hagar affirms that God "sees" her, God sees all of us and does not allow us to struggle alone!

Women who wrestle with faith and who have doubts and questions are not faithless. They are honest, and they refuse to live the façade that life is perfect when you find God. They understand God to be big enough to handle their wrestling, which is why they are more than likely to live their authentic truths.

Meditation Thought
When we pass through deep, confusing, and dangerous waters, God is with us.

Affirmation Statement
I am an overcomer! In my darkest hour, because God is with me, I shall prevail.

Prayer

Dear Lord, this week remind me that you have provided a safe place for me to wrestle with things I don't understand. Remind me that your love for me is constant and unwavering, even in moments I feel least loved.

Journal Reflections

_____

_____

_____

_____

_____

_____

_____

_____

_____

_____

_____

_____

_____

_____

_____

_____

_____

_____

_____

_____

_____

_____

_____

_____

_____

_____

Week 18

Lydia

Like a Boss

Acts 16

Scripture Focus

On the Sabbath we went outside the city gate to the river, where we expected to find a place of prayer. We sat down and began to speak to the women who had gathered there. One of those listening was a woman from the city of Thyatira named Lydia, a dealer in purple cloth. She was a worshiper of God. The Lord opened her heart to respond to Paul's message. When she and the members of her household were baptized, she invited us to her home. "If you consider me a believer in the Lord," she said, "come and stay at my house." And she persuaded us. (*Acts 16:13–15, NIV*)

Reflection

All we need to know about Lydia to bestow upon her the phrase "Like a Boss" is found in this brief biography. These few lines signal that in the areas of family, faith, social standing, and business, Lydia operates and functions as a woman at the helm—an independent, well-balanced woman in charge of her own life and navigating her own destiny. Her life story is another powerful reminder to women that living an abundantly free life, full of every desire you hold near, dear, and sacred, is achievable.

The phrase "Like a Boss" is not given to women who are bossy and domineering, nor reserved for women of a certain status and wealth. It is a tittle befitting women whose skill, confidence, and drive makes us take notice and thrust them into an undeniable place among those we respect, admire, and celebrate.

Lydia is a successful businesswoman in the profitable and well-paying purple cloth retail industry. Her clients are the rich and noble. Her business is so successful that it affords her a home large enough to need staff and spacious enough to offer hospitality to visitors. She is also active in the women's empowerment circle and has a known reputation as a woman who worships God. Her biography alone, however, isn't why Lydia is being celebrated here. It is her persuasive skill and her ability to get things done that catapults her to boss-like status.

Women who ascend to boss-like status have a knack for getting things done in a way that isn't belittling and isn't overbearing. This is why they are admired and respected. True bosses know how to move and inspire people to get the desired outcome without exciting fear, threats, and hovering on the borderline abusing power.

We see a possible glimpse of Lyida's tact as a boss when Paul says, "she persuaded us" in response to her invitation of hospitality. She said to them, "If you consider me a believer in the Lord, come and stay at my house." She made them an offer they couldn't refuse by attaching her offer to her faith. This is a woman who applies skill, tact, and wisdom to get a preferred outcome.

Lydia not only persuades Paul to be a guest in her home, but she convinces her entire household to be baptized and take additional steps in fully accepting the faith to which they were previously introduced. It takes boss-like skill to persuade others to buy into your ideas and ways of thinking.

Along with being persuasive, Lydia appears to be a social team player who meets with women regularly, an astute listener, and she is receptive and open to new ideas about faith and baptism that she had not yet heard. These are the skills of a woman who is leading and excelling in business, faith, family, and her social standing. Any woman who possesses a set of skills like these in her toolbox and deploys them tactfully is and will always function like a boss. These are women who are destined to live more abundantly free.

Meditation Thought

"True success isn't about how much money you make, it's about the difference you make in someone else's life."—Michelle Obama

Affirmation Statement

I am called to lead and I will lead with grace, skill, and tact.

Prayer

Dear Lord, this week help me to use every gift and skill you've given me to be a convincing witness for you in this world.

Journal Reflections

_____
_____
_____
_____
_____
_____
_____
_____
_____
_____
_____
_____
_____
_____
_____
_____

Poor Widow

My Two Cents Counts

Mark 12

Scripture Focus

Jesus sat down opposite the place where the offerings were put and watched the crowd putting their money into the temple treasury. Many rich people threw in large amounts. But a poor widow came and put in two very small copper coins, worth only a few cents. Calling his disciples to him, Jesus said, "Truly I tell you, this poor widow has put more in the treasury than all the others. They all gave out of their wealth; but she, out of her poverty, put in everything—all she had to live on." (Mark 12:41–44, NIV)

Reflection

If there was ever a woman in the Bible who reminds women that what we have to offer counts and counts significantly, it's this poor widow. She reminds women that no matter how seemingly small and insignificant our contribution may appear, it is worth just as much—if not more, according to Jesus—as anyone else's. When this poor widow puts her two cents in and is affirmed and lifted up by Jesus over and above everyone else, it is a reminder to women that our contributions are valuable.

We learn from this widow's story to not see the contributions we make in this world as small. Her story is an invaluable reminder that that what we contribute has a weight beyond monetary value, especially when we, like this widow, contribute from the core and essence of who we are.

At her core, this widow loved God and was a faithful servant. And to contribute to the world from such a place within us means we're adding value to the world.

Too often women's contributions are devalued and our voices silenced and ignored. Recently in our government our voices were left out of attempts to craft a new health-care bill. In churches, women's voices are often left out and silenced in the role of pastor and other important leadership positions. And in business, women's voices too often go unheard at high executive/management levels. But as this poor widow drops her two coins in the offering, and as Jesus referenced her offering as the most significant, it is a strong reminder that our contributions matter and they don't go unnoticed.

Her story reminds women of three very important points. She reminds us that our contributions are being accurately documented, that God is the only one who can rate and deem the worthiness of a contribution, and last but not least, her story reminds us never to make the mistake of comparing our contribution to others'. Comparison is the thief of joy. Trying to match ourselves with others will only contribute to seeing ourselves through a diminished lens. Because the one who judges accurately is keeping tabs, our focus only needs to be concerned with the generous, genuine giving of ourselves. This kind of giving is enough, it is sufficient, and it is overwhelmingly preferred!

In the same way Jesus watched to see what each person contributed and made an assessment of its worth, Jesus is still watching. If we generously give from the cores and essences of who we are, it's worth more than the wealth of this world.

Women who give their two cents and understand that their overall contribution to the world matters are women much like this widow, who was authentic in her giving and unbothered by what those around her gave or didn't give.

Meditation Thought

Never shrink back from adding your two cents, your opinions, and your voice. The world will either be positively shaped by your valuable contribution or less of what it could be from your silence.

Affirmation Statement

My genuine and authentic contributions to the world are priceless and can never be fully measured by the metrics of this world.

Prayer

Dear Lord, this week help me never fear making my contribution to the world.

Remind me that my voice and my opinions, if given out of my genuine love for you and my service to you, not only matter, but are priceless.

Journal Reflections

_____
_____
_____
_____
_____
_____
_____
_____
_____
_____
_____
_____
_____
_____
_____
_____
_____
_____
_____

Week 20

Leah

Digging in a Dry Place

Genesis 29

Scripture Focus

When the Lord saw that Leah was not loved, he enabled her to conceive, but Rachel remained childless. Leah became pregnant and gave birth to a son. She named him Reuben, for she said, "It is because the Lord has seen my misery. Surely my husband will love me now." She conceived again, and when she gave birth to a son she said, "Because the Lord heard that I am not loved, he gave me this one too." So she named him Simeon. Again she conceived, and when she gave birth to a son she said, "Now at last my husband will become attached to me, because I have borne him three sons." So she named him Levi. She conceived again, and when she gave birth to a son she said, "This time I will praise the Lord." So she named him Judah. The she stopped having children. (*Gen. 29:31–35, NIV*)

Reflection

Leah's story is the all-too-familiar story of a woman desperately trying to win a man's attention, love, and devotion. Her story is the quintessential story of every woman who has ever gone too far, given too much, or even groveled just a little to win the affections of a man who would not and/or could not reciprocate. Leah's story is reminiscent of contemporary stories of women who stay in loveless relationships beyond the expiration date hoping, to no avail, to receive the love they so freely give. Women, like Leah, who dig in dry relationship places hoping to find a nurturing spring of love will never live authentically and abundantly free.

If I were a gambling woman, I would bet that you would be hard pressed to find a woman who has not, at some point or another, sacrificed her soul and spirit at the altar of an unworthy man. If this isn't true of us, it is true of a woman we know. It is the familiar story of women who love emotionally unavailable men—men who are incapable of real intimacy and connections. It's the gone-viral and overshared story of women who make attempts to love others without first fully loving themselves, which is what causes women to land in the same place as Leah, unloved and devalued.

Leah's painful story reminds women of the insanity in trying to make men love us. She reminds us of the years we can waste making excuses and giving endless chances to men who don't deserve our faithful and undying love. But Leah's story also serves as a remedy to the insanity—if we take heed.

Because God knew Leah was unloved, God opened other doors for her to experience other expressions of love. Perhaps these other opportunities to love would help Leah recognize what love should feel like so she could stop expecting to get blood out of the turnip of Jacob's love. God's plan eventually worked, but not before it helped me see all years I ignored other expressions of love that God would send me as I hopelessly dug in dry wells of my own. God sees when we are unloved, but unless we see it, we'll keep hopelessly digging.

If we want to live the happy and abundant free lives God desires for us, we have to first make sure the love we have for ourselves is a well that runs over. Only when we drench ourselves in self-love will we have the ability to discern a love that will constantly takes from a love that reciprocates.

Women who seek to have relationships that are mutually validating, supportive, and loving must first nurture these things internally. A healthy sense of self-love is what will help us avoid unhealthy partnerships.

Women who fully embrace the greatest commandment to love our neighbors *as* we love our selves are women who will more than likely have meaningful relationships to accompany them as they journey the path of authentic and abundant living.

Meditation Statement

"It's all about falling in love with yourself and sharing that love with someone who appreciates you, rather than looking for love to compensate a self-love deficit."—Author Unknown

Affirmation

My actions, thoughts, decisions, and choices will reflect the deep love and care I give to myself. I will love myself with the same love I so freely give to others.

Prayer

Dear Lord, this week help me to always see myself as valuable and worthy of love. Help me to recognize and reject any form of love that is not supportive, compassionate, caring, and deserving of who I am.

Journal Reflections

_____
_____
_____
_____
_____
_____
_____
_____
_____
_____

Week 21

Hannah

I Need More

1 Samuel 1

Scripture Focus

There was a certain man from Ramathaim, a Zuphite from the hill country of Ephraim, whose name was Elkanah son of Jeroham, the son of Elihu, the son of Tohu, the son of Zuph, and Ephraimite. He had two wives; one was called Hannah and the other Peninnah. Peninnah had children, but Hannah had none. Year after year this man went up from his town to worship and sacrifice to the Lord Almighty at Shiloh, where Hophni and Phineahas, the two sons of Eli, where priests of the Lord. Whenever the day came for Elkanah to sacrifice, he would give portions of the meat to his wife Peninnah and to all her sons and daughters. But to Hannah he gave a double portion because he loved her, and the Lord had closed her womb. Because the Lord had closed Hannah's womb, her rival kept provoking her in order to irritate her. This went on year after year. Whenever Hannah went up to the house of the Lord, her rival provoked her till she wept and would not eat. Her husband Elkanah would say to her,

"Hannah, why are you weeping? Why don't you eat? Why are you downhearted? Don't I mean more to you than ten sons?" (1 Sam. 1:1–8, NIV)

Reflection

While there is a lot in Hannah's story to encourage women, the most helpful is how she destroys the notions that a man or a significant other is the be-all and end-all of what will satisfy and make women happy and fulfilled in life. Hannah shatters the idea that culture, faith, and family has tried to etch in the minds of women for centuries, that a truly satisfying life begins for women when we connect, fall in love, and marry our "soul mate." Her story reminds women to not make the mistake of believing that a man will be enough to make your life full and complete.

Hannah is a married woman who has a husband that loves and adores her and who makes an effort to show his affection. But while a great love is a significant compliment to life, it's only part of what makes for a satisfying and complete life. This is made clear when Hannah's husband's attempt to lift her from her sorrowful state fails and he asked her, "Don't I mean more to you than ten sons?"

There is no response to this question from Hannah, but the fact that she kept pursuing what she needed to satisfy and fulfill the deep longings of her soul says it all. Hannah had a deep longing to be a mother, and the love of a good man wasn't enough to make her forget this desire.

The same is true of women today. We may not have strong desires to be mothers like Hannah, but there are other needs we have that can't and won't be met through a significant other. There are dreams and desires for businesses, career opportunities, ministries, and so on that our relationships won't satisfy and that no matter how loving and nurturing they are, can't fulfill.

Hannah's story teaches women the valuable lesson of not losing ourselves and not forgetting what we want out of life, especially after we've found a significant other. She reminds us that being appreciative of the love we have doesn't mean we have to forsake the other parts of us that desire other things.

What's most encouraging about Hannah's story is she wasn't looking for her husband to fulfill the need she had. She was looking to God. Hannah was realistic about what needs her husband could fulfill in her life and the needs she had to rely on God to fulfill. Women need this kind of understanding and balance when we partner in relationships because without it, we can make the mistake of dethroning God in our lives and begin looking to a man to fulfill all our hopes and dreams.

Hannah reminds women that relationships are great, especially when you have one that is loving and supportive like the one she had. But she also reminds us to not put all our eggs in a relationship basket. There are needs and desires women have that can't be fulfilled through partnering with people.

Women who live fully satisfying lives are women who look to their Divine relationship, not a romantic relationships, for complete fulfillment.

Motivation Thought

People aren't designed to be our everything or supply our every need. God is.

Affirmation Statement

I will not lose myself or my desires when I'm in relationship, nor will I expect a relationship to fulfill my every need.

Prayer

Dear Lord, this week help me remember to keep romantic/love relationships in perspective. Help me avoid putting unrealistic expectations on my relationships and to look to you for a completely satisfying life.

Journal Reflections

_____

_____

_____

_____

_____

_____

_____

_____

_____

Week 22

Abigail

The "but" Between

1 Samuel 25:1-41

Scripture Focus

A certain man in Maon, who had property there at Carmel, was very wealthy. He had a thousand goats and three thousand sheep, which he was shearing in Carmel. His name was Nabal and his wife's name was Abigail. She was an intelligent and beautiful woman, but her husband was surly and mean in his dealings—he was a Calebite. (*1 Sam. 25:2, NIV*)

Reflection

Abigail is brought to us described as an intelligent and beautiful woman. However, immediately after her glowing description, we are warned of the glaring contradiction where her husband is concerned. The word "but" interjects and informs us to be prepared for a drastic departure from the glowing description Abigail is given. She is intelligent and beautiful, but he is surly and mean. This contradiction begs the question, "How does an intelligent woman ends up with a mean man whose name literally means fool (verse 25)?"

Abigail, like most women of her day, probably had little say in choosing the man she would end up with, so this question isn't posed to her. It's a question for modern women who have man-picking privileges. How is it that we as women sometimes end up in relationships where a "but" sharply separates our quality from the significant other we've picked?

Perhaps it's the proverbial list we've assembled of the man we desire. Most women I know, at some point in life, created a list of things we wanted our significant other to possess. This list may have included salary, height/weight, race, education, and faith requirements. It could have included tall, dark, and handsome requirements. It could have required the person to have never married, have no children, or at least no baby-mama drama. However, it's proven that we can get every item checked on our list and still end up, like Abigail, with a fool!

The world is in no short supply of educated fools, handsome fools, and in the case where Abigail is concerned, wealthy fools!

To avoid getting stuck with a "but" between the quality of woman we are and the quality of man we select, we have to not focus so much on how someone looks on paper, but rather how they show up for us in real life! More than a list of achievements and accomplishments, we need to consider if the person is supportive of our God-given gifts, talents, and callings. We have to consider if the person genuinely cares about our well-being. We have to consider if they bring to the table compassion and compromise. In other words, we have to look beyond the paper and beneath the fine, handsome, well-dressed specimen of man before us.

Having such a big "but" between two people trying to do life together can be catastrophic. Like Abigail's, the wrong significant other can cause misery and pose real danger. When you read the rest of Abigail's story, you will see that she was forced to clean up his messes and compensate for his shortcomings. I'm sure this made for some very miserable and lonely days. His short-sightedness and lack of generosity also nearly cost Abigail and her entire household their lives.

Abigail is another defiant woman who took matters into her own hands, which led her to securing a better future for herself. Her story is also another cautionary tale for women to be mindful of just how costly and dangerous it is for us to get into relationships with those who contradict rather than complement our core values.

Women who look beyond the superficial and the surface, women who use their partner-picking privileges to secure relationships that complement the values we hold dear, are women who are destined to live as close to "happily ever after" as one can get.

Motivation Thought

Chose your relationships wisely. Being alone will never cause as much loneliness as being in the wrong relationship.

Affirmation Statement

My relationships will reflect my core truth, that I am a woman of great worth and great intelligence.

Prayer

Dear Lord, this week help me evaluate my relationships. If changes are required, give me the strength to make them. If severing a relationship is required, give me the strength to end it. Most importantly, give me the wisdom to know the difference.

Journal Reflections

_____

_____

_____

_____

_____

_____

_____

_____

_____

_____

_____

Zipporah

Choices that Cut Deep

Exodus 4:18-26

Scripture Focus

> *At a lodging place on the way, the Lord met Moses and was about to kill him. But Zipporah took a flint knife, cut off her son's foreskin and touched Moses' feet with it. "Surely you are a bridegroom of blood to me," she said. So the Lord let him alone. (Exod. 4:24–25, NIV)*

Reflection

If you've ever been between a rock and a hard place or if you've ever had to make a decision between two seemingly bad options, you have been where we find Zipporah. Zipporah was forced to make the difficult decision of allowing her son to experience excruciating pain that she, herself, inflicted on him, or allow her husband to die.

Most of us would rather cut off our hands than inflict pain on those we love, but there are times there's no way of avoiding rock-and-hard-place choices. If you've ever had to make the decision to cut off a drug-addicted/substance-abusing loved one, it was a rock-and-hard-place choice. If you had to report a loved one for the sexual assault against another family member, it was a rock-and-hard-place choice. If you had to end the financial support of a loved one because you realized you had become an enabler preventing him or her from standing on his or her own two feet, it was a rock-and-hard-place choice.

I'm sure, like Zipporah, when faced with these decision there was a wrestling with guilt. When we contribute to the pain of others, especially those we love, guilt is inevitable. Along with guilt there comes a barrage of questions. Is there another way? Have all other possibilities been exhausted? Hurting a loved one, even for the right reasons, has to be one of the most difficult decisions we will ever have to make.

One could say that Zipporah was comforted in knowing the pain was temporary. But I'm sure as she heard her son scream in agony, this was of little consolation. The cut Zipporah gave her son was deeply felt by both of them. His pain had to cut straight to her heart. We can see a glimpse of her pain as she throws her son's foreskin at her husband's feet.

Sometimes there are no easy answers, only hard choices, even for people of faith.

What Zipporah's story does for us is remind us to consider the long game. The pain she allowed in the present prevented a more dreadful future.

Like Zipporah, women today are not without having to make painful decisions. Life will constantly present us with rock-and-hard-place choices that will require us to experience a present pain to avoid a more fatal future.

Women who are strong enough to make tough choices are the women who are destined to live bold and free.

Meditation Thought
Sometimes the hardest thing and the right thing are the same thing.

Affirmation Statement
I will trust my God, my faith, and myself in every difficult decision.

Prayer

Dear Lord, this week remind me to listen for you and invite your guidance in every decision I make, especially the tough decisions. Help me to not make decisions out of fear, but rather out of the sound mind you have given me.

Journal Reflections

_____
_____
_____
_____
_____
_____
_____
_____
_____
_____
_____
_____
_____
_____
_____
_____
_____
_____
_____
_____
_____
_____
_____
_____
_____
_____
_____
_____

Week 24

Martha

Scripture Focus

As Jesus and his disciples were on their way, he came to a village where a woman named Martha opened her home to him. She had a sister called Mary, who sat at the Lord's feet listening to what he had said. But Martha was distracted by all the preparations that had to be made. She came to him and asked, "Lord, don't you care that my sister has left me to do the work by myself? Tell her to help me!" "Martha, Martha," the Lord answered, "you are worried and upset about many things, but few things are needed—or indeed one. Mary has chosen what is better, and it will not be taken from her." (Luke 10:38–4, NIV)

Reflection

It's one thing when women have to fight an entire cultural and social structure just to walk in their own chosen paths, but it's a whole other thing when women have to fight this same fight with other women.

There is nothing more disheartening than women who assist the "system" in keeping women in their perceived "place." There is nothing more heartbreaking than women who limit other women to their own ideals of what women should be and do. And whether women do this consciously (out of hate and spite) or unconsciously (from drinking way too much of the social and cultural Kool-Aid), it's a painful experience for women on the receiving end.

Support and encouragement from other women as we brave new frontiers is critical. Encouraging a sister to live her own life, chart her own course, and navigate new terrain is vital to the entire sisterhood. But when we receive discouragement in place of encouragement, it makes the womanhood journey more difficult.

We aren't sure what Martha's feelings were when she confronted Jesus about what Mary should be doing. Perhaps Mary's desire to grow and avail herself of something new and outside of what she was normally used to made Martha feel as if she were being left behind. Perhaps Martha's desire to see Mary stay in the same place was from her own insecurities and her own lack of ambition. Either way, Jesus confirms for Martha that Mary will not be held back and forced to remain in a perceived place. He affirms that Mary has every right to decide for herself what's best for her.

Martha's embedded beliefs about women convinced her that her sister was out of place, but Jesus didn't agree. Jesus reminded Martha, and her story reaffirms for us how important it is for women to give other women permission to live free of our expectations and limitations. Jesus didn't side with Martha about the path her sister chose. Jesus affirmed Mary's choice in stepping off the path of what was expected of her.

Jesus let her live!

Women who fearlessly embrace new paths and who are open to occupying nontraditional spaces are the women who are destined to live authentically free.

Meditation Thought

Enjoy the pace and journey of your own life. Others may be doing more and further along and that's OK! Your journey is for you!

Affirmation Statement

I will not make it my goal to walk in footsteps already marked. My authentic journey begins with me!

Prayer

Dear Lord, this week help me to focus on the life you're calling me to live. Help me to not be influenced or scared off the path that leads to the life I was meant to live.

Journal Reflections

_____

_____

_____

_____

_____

_____

_____

_____

_____

_____

_____

_____

_____

_____

_____

_____

_____

_____

_____

_____

_____

_____

Week 25

Manoah's Wife

You Are Capable

Judges 13

Scripture Focus

God listened to Manoah, and the angel of God came again to the woman while she sat in the field; but her husband Manoah was not with her. So the woman ran quickly and told her husband, "The man who came to me the other day has appeared to me." Manoah got up and followed his wife, and came to the man and said to him, "Are you the man who spoke to this woman?" And he said, "I am." Then Manoah said, "Now when your words come true, what is to be the boy's rule of life; what is he to do?" The angel of the LORD said to Manoah, "Let the woman give heed to all that I said to her. (Judg. 13:9–13, NRSV)

Reflection

M anoah's wife, the mother of Sampson, is hardly ever mentioned in church sermons and studies today. She is one of the least known biblical characters, yet her story remains one of the most powerful and encouraging stories for women. Her story is a reminder of how God views women as the capable, qualified, and competent vessels God intentionally uses in Divine plans that impact and change the world. Her story speaks loudly and clearly to anyone who has ever questioned whether God just uses women by default. This is an account of God's preference for speaking directly to a woman—even when there was a capable man available.

God speaks directly to Manoah's wife and informs her of the son she shall have. God instructs her how to care for herself during pregnancy, how to care for the boy once he's born, and the plan and purpose God has in store for the boy. It is quite possible that upon hearing this news that Manoah's wife was not comfortable with God coming directly to her, which may be why she ran to get her husband the second time the angel appeared to her. Perhaps she had been conditioned to believe, like some people in churches today, that God doesn't speak to women directly. But when she does runs to her husband, the angel redirects her husband back to his wife.

This was perhaps God's sign and confirmation to Manoah's wife that she was very capable of hearing from God and following through with his instructions, and that God was intentionally seeking her out to be the leader on this Divine mission. This is also a confirmation that women unfortunately still need today.

As sexism continues to be woven securely in the fabric of many of our institutions, women need to be reminded that God didn't create us to be a second-class, default gender. In a world where women are so devalued that they earn less money for the same work and where female leadership is still dismal in most industries, women need be affirmed and confirmed as capable, competent, and qualified to do anything we set our hearts and minds to do.

God confirming to Manoah and redirecting him back to what the angel spoke to his wife is an encouraging reminder of how God is no respecter of genders. God doesn't prefer one gender over another. God doesn't see men as stronger and more usable than women because the success of any Divine mission is not dependent upon the vessel, but the One who uses the vessel.

Women who believe they are capable, competent, and qualified to do and be anything—even in the Kingdom of God—are women who will be used by God to help level the playing field. These are women who will live authentically free.

Meditation Thought

Women are also made in the image of God and therefore women too are God's preferred choice.

Affirmation Statement

I am chose by God. I am capable, brave, and significant even in those moments it feels like I'm not.

Prayer

Dear Lord, this week help me to remember how fearfully and wonderfully you've made me. Help me to move forward accepting every assignment, challenge, and opportunity, knowing that I am capable, competent, and qualified.

Journal Reflections

_____

_____

_____

_____

_____

_____

_____

_____

_____

_____

_____

_____

_____

_____

_____

_____

_____

Week 26
Woman In the Crowd

Give Her Some Credit

Luke 11

Scripture Focus

As Jesus was saying this, a woman in the crowd raised her voice and said to him, "Blessed is the womb that bore you and the breasts that nursed you." (Luke 11:27, NRSV)

⌣

Reflection

There is nothing more encouraging and empowering than seeing women celebrate, support, and lift up other women. There is nothing that shows a woman who is confident and comfortable in her own skin like one who is able to give props, credit, and kudos to another deserving woman. This is the example set by this nameless woman in the Gospel of Luke.

While Jesus is in the midst of teaching a large crowd and using parables to explain the deep truths of the Kingdom of God in such a way that men, women, boys, and girls can understand, this woman is so profoundly impressed that she screams out and praises Jesus's mother. This woman isn't taking anything away from Jesus, she is simply acknowledging and giving credit to the woman who played a significant role in Jesus's life. As a woman herself, and possibly a mother, she understood the nurture, care, and sacrifices women have to make for their children—and with this understanding she felt it necessary to affirm Jesus's mother and the role she played in this incredible gift she brought to the world.

Beyond affirming Jesus's mother, I'm sure her sentiment resonated with other women standing in the crowd. When one woman is praised and lifted up for her accomplishments, other women who have achieved similar goals are able to feel their own sense of value. In this male-dominated world, it is so necessary for women to support and praise other women for achieving goals, for reaching milestones, and even for small everyday victories.

There is a lie and a myth that is perpetuated that women can't get along. I personally reject this lie. While it is true that we have, in the sisterhood, mean-girl cliques, women who boast of only having male friends because women are too catty, and women who operate from a place of scarcity who believe there is only room for one woman at the table so they sabotage other women to keep their place, these are not a representation of the true sisterhood, nor do they reflect the majority.

Women like the nameless woman who had no problem giving Jesus's mother credit are not in competition with any other woman because they understand that the God we serve has room enough for all God's daughters to shine.

We should celebrate that this woman screams out praise for Jesus's mother. We should also model her sentiment and give credit and praise to other women when they play significant roles in achieving great victories like Jesus's mother, as well as when small victories are won. After all, win is a win!

Women who are intentional about supporting, encouraging, and lifting other women clearly understand that when one woman rises, all women rise—even if just a little.

Meditation Thought

Behind every successful woman is a tribe of other successful women who have her back.

Affirmation Statement

I am not an insecure woman; therefore I don't compete with other women. I am a secure woman, and therefore I compliment and encourage other women.

Prayer

Dear Lord, this week remind me that I am my sister's keeper. Help me to be a supporter and encourager of all the women who are in my sphere of influence.

Journal Reflections

_____
_____
_____
_____
_____
_____
_____
_____
_____
_____
_____
_____
_____
_____
_____
_____
_____
_____
_____
_____
_____
_____
_____

Daughters of Philip

Single and Killing It

Acts 21

Scripture Focus

> *The next day we left and came to Caesarea; and we went into the house of Philip the evangelist, one of the seven, and stayed with him. He had four unmarried daughters who had the gift of prophecy.* (Acts 21:8–9, NRSV)

Reflection

We may not have many details about Philip's four daughters, but the two details we are given are enough to remind women that singleness is not a curse and that we are gifted and equipped to enjoy and fully embrace every stage of life.

We don't know why their marital status is included in their brief biography. Perhaps it's because women were measured or valued by marriage. Perhaps respectability came through marriage. What's important is their single status is just background noise to the louder announcement that these women were gifted prophets!

Whether women are single or single again after divorce, these daughters remind us that a single life and a gifted life can be one and the same! They remind us that there is more to life than being married and that singleness doesn't prevent us from living passionate lives. These women were gifted, and nothing brings you more passion than operating and walking in your gift.

These single sisters remind women not to put our lives on hold waiting for a relationship with a significant other. They remind us to saddle up on life and ride! Their story says to us that all on our own and without the help of a significant other we can make our mark on this world. They remind us that as solo individuals we are enough and that we have been given gifts that will help us create happy, fulfilled, and satisfied lives.

We don't know if these sisters would eventually get married or whether they were content in their singleness. We don't know if they took Paul's teaching to heart and decided that they would never marry (1 Corinthians 7:8). We don't know if they were so busy building their careers as prophets that they decided to put marriage on the back burner until they established themselves—I'm sure it was a huge undertaking establishing themselves as bona fide prophets. The point is, at the time of this passage, they were single, gifted, and living out their purpose.

Women who understand that there is a kind of happiness, passion, and fulfillment that we can only get through using our gifts are women who are living authentically free.

Meditation Thought
Creating a satisfied, happy, and fulfilling life begins with connecting with your passion, not a person.

Affirmation Statement
I am a complete and whole individual. My life, purpose, and happiness do not hinge on the relationship box I check.

Prayer

Dear Lord, this week if there is any place in me that is not content, happy, and whole, remind me that it is my responsibility to find and fill those places. Remind me that you have given me everything I need to live a happy and satisfied life.

Journal Reflections

_____
_____
_____
_____
_____
_____
_____
_____
_____
_____
_____
_____
_____
_____
_____
_____
_____
_____
_____
_____
_____
_____
_____
_____
_____
_____
_____

Week 28

Women at Calvary

Squad Goals

Matthew 27:45-55

Scripture Focus

Many women were also there, looking on from a distance: they had followed Jesus from Galilee and provided for him. (Luke 27:55, NIV)

⌒‿⌒

Reflection

If ever there was a group of women I envy and would wholeheartedly welcome in my sisterhood circle of friends, it would be the women found at the foot of the cross when Jesus died. These women prove to be the kind of women you want on your team, in your corner, and covering your back.

We often hear about the twelve male disciples, and we know most of them by name, but Jesus had many disciples who were women. They were with him from the beginning of his ministry when he started in Galilee, they were there at the cross, and they were the first to witness the resurrection. These are the kind of women every woman needs in her life.

Like the women at Calvary, we need ride-or-die women in our lives. They were with Jesus during the highs and lows. When he fed five thousand people and healed the sick, these women were there; when he was about to breathe his last breath, they were still there. Through thick and thin, these women were there. They were a ride-or-die group of women who never dropped the ball.

They teach us what real squad goals look like. We learn from these women what it means to be supportive, but not be overbearing. They watched Jesus from a distance as he hung on the cross. They had little power to change the situation, but they knew that a ministry of presence was powerful, reassuring, and needed. This is a powerful reminder that when you have a caring and connected circle of sisters, words aren't always needed. Presence is enough. Looking up and seeing a good sister girlfriend in your deepest moment of sorrow can often do more than verbal expressions. Just knowing a sister is there for you can be the best medicine.

But these women weren't just emotionally there for Jesus, they met the physical needs too. The women of Calvary followed Jesus and provided for him and the other disciples (Luke 8:1–3) out of their very own resources. A good squad is never OK when one squad member is struggling. They will pool resources together to make sure that no squad member is left behind or out in the cold. A good squad makes sure everyone in the circle's needs are met.

Even when squad members don't agree, which is likely with any squad, they are still supportive. Good squads fight fair, forgive quickly, and avoid dragging the names and the transgressions of others sisters through the mud.

Women need to have these kinds of women in their circles, but more importantly we need to be these kinds of women in our circle. We need the be the kind of sister, woman, friend that we want other women to be to us.

When women come together with the understanding that we are better together, that we go further together, and that we can accomplish more together, we will affect real change in the world and create safer spaces, more opportunities, and strong support so women can thrive.

Women who create sisterhood circles that are supportive of other women are vital to bringing the Kingdom of God on earth as it is in heaven—these women are not just concerned that they live authentically free, they also want to ensure all women in their influence live the same.

Meditation Thought

"A circle of women may be the most powerful force known to humanity. If you have one, embrace it. If you need one, seek it. If you find one, dive in, hold on, and love it up."—Author Unknown

Affirmation Statement

I am at my best when I'm loving, supporting, and encouraging my sisters just as I love, support, and encourage myself.

Prayer

Dear Lord, this week help me to be the kind of woman and sister friend that other women need. Help me to model the love and encouragement to other women that I know I need myself.

Journal Reflections

_____
_____
_____
_____
_____
_____
_____
_____
_____
_____
_____
_____
_____
_____
_____
_____
_____
_____

Week 29

Widow of Zarephath

Our Reality versus God's Truth

1 Kings 17:8-16

Scripture Focus

> *Then the word of the Lord came to [Elijah]: "Go at once to Zarephath in the region of Sidon and stay there. I have directed a widow there to supply you with food." So he went to Zarephath. When he came to the town gate, a widow was there gathering sticks. He called to her and asked, "Would you bring me a little water in a jar so I may have a drink?" As she was going to get it, he called, "And bring me, please, a piece of bread." "As surely as the Lord your God lives," she replied, "I don't have any bread—only a handful of flour in a jar and a little olive oil in a jug. I am gathering a few sticks to take home and make a meal for myself and my son, that we may eat it—and die."* (1 Kings 17:8–12, NIV)

Reflection

The widow of Zarephath is the woman who reminds us to see ourselves the way God sees us—and to remember that our reality is no match for God's truth. Her story is a contradiction of epic proportions that should remind every woman that God has a plan for our lives that will not only bless and sustain us, but will allow us to be a blessing to others.

Most of us have been through periods in life where we look at how far we are from the life we set out to live. Oftentimes, the life we dreamed looks nothing like the life we are actually living. During these times it's easy to question ourselves and see ourselves as less than who we really are. But these are actually the times to position ourselves to see from another angle—to see from God's vantage point.

God was completely aware that the woman God assigned to supply the prophet Elijah with food had no food. Yet God saw her as a supplier of food. God sees women today the same way.

At this present moment you may not have the resources, income, education, or dream career that you desire. In fact, it may seem totally out of reach and unlikely, but this widow's story reminds us of the kind of faith we must stir up when we encounter these moments. She remind us to see our reality, but trust God's truth.

This widow was at the end of her rope, but not the end of her hope. She was low on food, but not on faith. When Elijah told her what God said, she trusted and followed through, and God made lasting provisions for her and her son.

This widow reminds women that when we are only able to see ourselves through our own circumstances, we are looking from the wrong perspective. We have to trust that what we see is no match for what God has said will happen in us, through us, and with us. God always has more in store for us that we can visually see with our naked eyes.

Women who see themselves the way God sees them, regardless of how hopeless the circumstance, are women destined to see God transform their limited reality into abundance.

Meditation Thought

Whatsoever things are lovely and true, think on these things, see these things, and believe these things. God is still transforming lives.

Affirmation Statement

There is more to me than meets the eye. I am more than my current circumstances. I am the beautiful creation that God envisioned at my conception.

Prayer

Dear Lord, this week help me to not focus so much on what I see that I forget what you see. Remind me that the path you've called me to journey requires that I walk by faith and not by sight.

Journal Reflections

_____

_____

_____

_____

_____

_____

_____

_____

_____

_____

_____

_____

_____

_____

_____

_____

_____

_____

_____

_____

_____

_____

_____

_____

Week 30

Women at the Tomb

Do It Afraid

Matthew 28:1-10

Scripture Focus

The angel said to the women, "Do not be afraid, for I know that you are looking for Jesus, who was crucified. He is not here; he has risen, just as he said. Come and see the place where he lay. Then go quickly and tell his disciples: 'He has risen from the dead and is going ahead of you into Galilee. There you will see him.' Now I have told you." So the women hurried away from the tomb, afraid yet filled with joy, and ran to tell his disciples. (Matt. 28:5–8, NIV)

Reflection

If you need—and we all do at times—a little inspiration to get yourself moving forward when fear has tried to keep you stagnant and still, you need look no further than the women found at the tomb the morning Jesus resurrected. These women will have you beating your chest and confronting every fear that has tried to hold you back from the joys you were meant to experience.

"They hurried away from the tomb, afraid yet filled with joy" is a such a powerful statement and should not be glanced over. These contradicting emotions are a reminder that some of the best experiences of life are often found on the other side of fear.

These women experienced both these emotions as they were instructed to go and tell the disciples the good news that Jesus had risen. This mission they were sent on made these women the very first preachers of the Gospel of Jesus Christ. And like most preachers I know, present company included, we fulfill this mission with complete joy, but we would be remiss if we didn't admit that fear too is always present. But their message to us is: do it afraid!

What these women feared is not actually mentioned. Perhaps they feared the unknown, which is most commonly feared. They didn't know what to expect with the Risen Jesus. It's possible they questioned and were a little anxious about what this new experience of Jesus might be like. Perhaps they feared going to tell the disciples. Perhaps they feared the disciples wouldn't believe them—which when you read the passage, they didn't. We aren't told why the women were afraid, only that they were afraid.

But their fear was minimized with joy. These women were afraid, but they were also filled with joy. They remind us that whatever we fill ourselves with will have the deepest impact on our outcomes.

Fear is par for any course that leads to destiny, passion, and purpose. It will always present itself in convincing ways when you are hurrying to fulfill your life's mission, like the women at the tomb.

Although fear was present with them, they were determined not to let it hold them back. Fear of what others thought, fear of failure, fear of the unknown, fear of being the first, fear of rejection—none of these fears kept these women from experiencing the joys God intended them because they were willing to fulfill their mission afraid.

Women who understand that there are some things we are going to have to do afraid and outside of our comfort zones are women who will experience the abundant joys life has to offer.

Meditation Thought

If we don't develop the courage to live our dreams, we will live our fears.

Affirmation Statement

I will courageously and fearlessly confront my fears so that my joy will be full.

Prayer

Dear Lord, this week help me to have a healthy relationship with fear. Help me to discern when fear is instinctively warning me of danger and alerting me to be cautious and when it is attempting to hold me back from what you have for me. Give me the courage to move forward when fear would keep me still.

Journal Reflections

_____
_____
_____
_____
_____
_____
_____
_____
_____
_____
_____
_____
_____
_____
_____
_____
_____
_____
_____
_____

Woman of Samaria

Don't Get Me Wrong

John 4:4-42

Scripture Focus

He told her, "Go, call your husband and come back." "I have no husband," she replied. Jesus said to her, "You are right when you say you have no husband. The fact is, you have had five husbands, and the man you now have is not your husband. What you have just said is quite true." (John 4:16–17, NIV)

Then leaving her water jar, the woman went back to the town and said to the people, "Come, see a man who told me everything I ever did. Could this be the Christ?" (John 4:28–29, NIV)

Reflection

One of the most important battles women have to fight is the battle against false labels that scar our reputation and cause us to be outcasts. This is the case with the woman in Samaria. She is a woman who is inaccurately labeled as sinful and immoral and whom before she encountered Jesus, was deserving of a biblical side-eye from those who read her story. But a closer look at the woman of Samaria reveals that she was, in fact, quite the opposite.

This was a woman of faith. She was a woman with worship on the forefront of her mind, which is evident as the first words out of her mouth to discuss with Jesus when she thought him to be a prophet were about worship. She was also one of the most effective witnesses for Jesus, which is evident as she successfully convinced her entire town to come see the Messiah.

Her story further confirms that an accurate rewriting and retelling of biblical history, especially where women are concerned, is always appropriate and needed. She reminds contemporary women that people will misjudge and misinterpret who we are, but our record, character, and witness will always speak volumes for us, revealing our truth. Her story is encouragement for women to not be too concerned with those who judge us on the surface, because what other people think about who we are can in no way hinder our work, witness, and even whether our names go down in history.

Because this woman had five husbands, the worst is assumed. However, because women had no control over marriage or divorce, it is more likely that her multiple marital status is attributed to the brother-in-law duties referenced in Deuteronomy 25:5–10 and Luke 20:27–33. This laws states that if a woman's husband dies, she is forbidden to remarry outside of her husband's family, and in order to secure an heir to carry on her deceased husband's name, she is expected to marry his brother. This is how a woman who has no power to divorce and remarry ends up with five husbands. It was legal and not in the least immoral.

The woman of Samaria has been misread, misinterpreted, and woefully mislabeled in the same way women of color have been. Sapphire, Mammy, and Jezebel come to mind as just a few of the negative stereotypes that have contributed to the misrepresentation and misinterpretation of women of color. Women of color have to fight such labels to be seen accurately, and this same fight must be waged against inaccurate portrayals of women in the Bible.

If she was such a sinful and immoral woman, would she have turned the conversation with Jesus to worship? If she was a known sinful and immoral woman, could she have effectively witnessed to those in her village about the Christ? Would they have accepted such witness from such a woman? Wouldn't the last person to convince them to come and see the Messiah be a sinful, immoral woman?

The woman of Samaria has been wrongfully shamed and dragged through history as an immoral example when she is actually a great example of a woman of God. Her story reminds us to take with a grain of salt and reject negative interpretations and representations of ourselves and other women. She reminds us also that people can misinterpret who we are but it can't prevent us from making an indelible mark on this world.

Women who demand accurate interpretations and representations of themselves and other women create safe and needed spaces in a world that is all too quick and content to misjudge. They create Kingdom environments where women aren't shackled and weighted down by what others believe them to be, and are free to soar in authenticity.

Meditation Thought

Men and those in the dominant culture decide 97 percent of the time how women are portrayed in media. This is both a warning and a fact.

Affirmation Statement

I will use my voice, my power, and my presence to reject every misrepresentation and misinterpretation of who I am in service to myself and to my fellow sisters.

Prayer

Dear Lord, this week help me to not wrongfully critique others and to reject the wrongful and inaccurate critiques of me.

Journal Reflections

_____
_____
_____
_____
_____
_____
_____
_____

Week 32

Tamar

Refuse to Live in Shame

2 Samuel 13:1-21

Scripture Focus

*Then Amnon said to Tamar, "Bring the food here into my bed-
room so I may eat from your hand." And Tamar took the bread
she had prepared and brought it to her brother Amnon in his
bedroom. But when she took it to him to eat, he grabbed her and
said, "Come to bed with me, my sister." "No, my brother!" she
said to him. "Don't force me! Such a thing should not be done in
Israel! Don't do this wicked thing. What about me? Where could
I get rid of my disgrace? And what about you? You would be like
one of those wicked fools in Israel. Please speak to the king; he
will not keep me from being married to you." But he refused to
listen to her, and since he was stronger than she, he raped her.* (2
Samuel 13:10–14, NIV)

*And Tamar lived in her brother Absalom's house, a desolate
woman.* (2 Samuel 13:20b, NIV)

Reflection

There is no better example of a victim being punished for a crime committed against her than the story of Tamar. She was not only the victim of a rape, but she was punished for her rape by being forced to live as a desolate woman for the rest of her life. Tamar's ancient story stands as a cautionary reminder to contemporary women of how little has changed when it comes to violence against women. Her story reminds women that we are still very much in an ongoing battle with a culture that blames, shames, and punishes women for the sexual abuse committed against us. Tamar's story is a powerful reminder that if women don't fight and win this battle, it will prevent us from living in the abundant freedom Jesus affords us.

Sexual violence against women and girls in the United States is staggering. The age a girl is first likely to be fondled in the United States is five years old. One out of every six women is victim of an attempted or a complete rape. At the hands of strangers, family members, and friends, millions of women and girls in the United States are raped, trafficked, molested, or experience some other form of sexual abuse. After this experience of violence, these women are not believed and are blamed or ignored, which results in them living, like Tamar, in shame and/or hiding.

After surviving a sexual assault, Tamar is then sentenced to live a "desolate life," a term used to indicate that she would live as a woman without the beautiful future she imagined for herself and in a permanent state of public humiliation. And like many women today, Tamar ends up the one suffering and locked in a life sentence of seclusion, rather than the one who committed violence against her.

As Tamar begs her brother not to rape her, she asks a very poignant question that I think if we answer, women will be less likely to live out life sentences in the shame prisons of this rape culture. Tamar asks, "Where could I get rid of my disgrace?" The simple answer to Tamar's question—and what women who've experienced sexual violence need to first know—is that the shame is not yours. The shame is on the person who committed the violation. Another important response to Tamar's question that women need to know is that shame lives in secrecy. Confide in someone you trust, someone who will help you understand that the toxic, ugly, violent act that was done to you does not poison you, therefore there is no reason to hide or feel guilty, embarrassed, or ashamed. More than Tamar needed her brother Absalom to avenged her, she needed him to encourage her not to hide and live in shame. Absalom should have told Tamar that she was not tarnished and less valuable and that she had no reason to live a desolate life. She needed him to say to her that she was not the ugly thing that happened to her. This would have helped her reject her shame prison and live in total freedom.

It's unfortunate that we live in a rape culture where women's bodies are preyed on and seen as fair game. It is discouraging that men with power like Harvey Weinstein, Bill Cosby, Bill O'Reilly, and Donald Trump, to name a few, suffer no real punishment for being sexual predators. What is most appalling, however, is that women are blamed, further victimized, and are often forced to live with a shroud of shame as a result of sexual violence.

Women who understand that sexual violence committed against women is not our shame to carry and who show compassion for other women by holding safe spaces where women can unlock the prison bars of a desolate life are defiant women. And women who show contempt for those who commit violence against women as well as a culture that permits violence against women are doing the real work to make the Kingdom of God a present reality.

These women make it possible for women to live in authentic and abundant freedom.

Motivation Thought
There is no disgrace in being a survivor of sexual assault. The disgrace belongs to the assaulter.

Affirmation Statement
I am not what happened to me. I am what I choose to become.

Prayer
Dear Lord, this week help me to fully embrace that I am I'm loved, worthy, and valued, no matter the circumstances of my life. Help me to understand that a life lived in seclusion and in isolation is not the life you have for me.

Journal Reflections

Week 33

Mary

Just Do You

Luke 10

Scripture Focus

As Jesus and his disciples were on their way, he came to a village where a woman named Martha opened her home to him. She had a sister called Mary, who sat at the Lord's feet listening to what he had said. But Martha was distracted by all the preparations that had to be made. She came to him and asked, "Lord, don't you care that my sister has left me to do the work by myself? Tell her to help me!" "Martha, Martha," the Lord answered, "you are worried and upset about many things, but few things are needed—or indeed one. Mary has chosen what is better, and it will not be taken from her." (Luke 10:38–4, NIV)

Reflection

Howard Thurman, theologian and civil rights leader, said, "If you cannot hear the sound of the genuine in you, you will all of your life spend your days at the ends of strings someone else pulls."

These powerful words were the impetus and for me living my authentic life. After hearing these words, the last thing I wanted—and the thing I thought to be most disrespectful and dishonoring to God—was to allow someone else to pull the strings in the life God had given me. Mary, in this passage, appears to feel the same way.

Mary rejected perceived expectations placed on her, and she followed the beat of her own drum. Ignoring the plans others had for her, she followed the sound of the genuine. In doing so she reminds modern women who seek to live abundantly and authentically free to refuse to allow culture norms and traditions to dictate their life's journey.

Intuition is a gift some women rarely use and some mistrust, but intuition is not to be ignored. It is our North Star home. Mary listened and followed her internal guide, which lead her to make the best possible choice for her life—a choice Jesus said was "better."

Mary's story is confirmation for women not to wait for an invitation or permission to pursue the desires of their hearts. She walked in alongside the disciples and took her seat at the table—a seat at Jesus's feet. She didn't seek approval or permission. And she was affirmed!

Another scholar of words, the singer and songwriter India Arie, has a quote that also inspires women on our journey to live free. She says, "It's time to peel back all the layers put between who you were meant to be and who you are...just go be who you are!" In other words, the real and authentic "us" can be buried under other people's opinions and expectations. And it is our job to discern and dig through those expectations to find the treasure of our authenticity.

Women who fearlessly pursue the desires of their hearts, who follow the sound of the genuine, and who refuse to allow others to dictate what life should look like for them are the women who have, in the words of Jesus, "chosen better."

Meditation Thought

"Just do you—somebody's got to be a star. Just do you—somebody's got to raise the bar. Just do you—somebody's got to change the game. Just do you today!"—India Arie

Affirmation Statement

I will listen internally for the sound of the genuine and freely dance to that rhythm.

Prayer

Dear Lord, this week help me to be guided by your internal voice. Help me to remember that I will always make better decisions for my life when I am true to myself and faithful to you.

Journal Reflections

_____
_____
_____
_____
_____
_____
_____
_____
_____
_____
_____
_____
_____
_____
_____
_____
_____
_____
_____
_____
_____
_____
_____

Week 34
Rizpah

Demand Dignity

2 Samuel 21:8-14

Scripture Focus

But the king took Armoni and Mephibosheth, the two sons of Aiah's daughter Rizpah, whom she had born to Saul, together with the five sons of Saul's daughter Merb, whom she had born to Adriel son of Barzillai the Meholaolathite. He handed them over to the Gibenoites, who killed them and exposed their bodies on a hill before the Lord. All seven of them fell together; they were put to death during the first days of the harvest, just as the barley harvest was beginning. Rizpah daughter of Aiah took sackcloth and spread it out for herself on a rock. From the beginning of the harvest till the rain poured down from the heavens on the bodies, she did not let the birds touch them by day or the wild animals by night. (2 Sam. 21:8–10, NIV)

Reflection

The story of Rizpah is reminiscent of the stories of the mothers who have lost sons to police-related killings of black youth, particularly Michael Brown, who was killed by police, his body left in the street for several hours. These mothers, like Rizpah, had to fight and continue to fight for the dignity and humanity of their children.

Rizpah's fight began when her sons were gruesomely executed, and their bodies hanged and left on a hill as a way to shame and humiliate the deceased. Like the young men we've lost to police brutality, Rizpah's sons committed no crime themselves—they were punished because of their heritage. Although Rizpah was powerless to prevent her sons from being killed, she was a powerful force in protecting and preserving their dignity in death. She refused to allow her sons to be seen as worthy of the death they endured. Night and day she fought off wild animals seeking to devour their bodies and stood as a one-woman vigil until her demand to give her sons a proper burial was met.

In many ways Rizpah reminds women—especially women of color—that being treated with dignity is never automatic and that when it is denied to us we must demand it. Whether we are demanding it for ourselves or demanding it collectively in state houses, church houses, and corporate settings across this nation where the collective fight for dignity is often waged, we must be as determined as Rizpah.

Rizpah reminds women that we must fight tooth and nail for respect that should be freely given. She reminds women of the risks we must take and what it will sometimes cost us to demand the respect we are owed. But dignity is—or should be—a core value for every woman, and there is no price too high to pay to secure it.

Women who demand to be treated with respect and dignity are women who are able to see their reflections in the mirror and beam with pride. These are women who are fearless in the fight to live free.

Meditation Thought

It is sinful to treat people without dignity; it is also unacceptable to tolerate such treatment from others.

Affirmation Statement

I am a woman of strength and courage, one who values herself and is willing to fight for the respect and dignity I deserve.

Prayer

Dear Lord, this week help me to be a fearless witness in this world that recognizes the value in all people. Help me to consistently wage war against those who reserve dignity and humane treatment for only a few.

Journal Reflections

_____

_____

_____

_____

_____

_____

_____

_____

_____

_____

_____

_____

_____

_____

_____

_____

_____

_____

_____

_____

_____

_____

_____

_____

_____

_____

Week 35

Naomi

Ruth 4:13-22

Scripture Focus

The women said to Naomi: "Praise be to the Lord, who this day has not left you without a guardian-redeemer. May he become famous throughout Israel! He will renew your life and sustain you in your old age. For your daughter-in-law who loves you and who is better to you than seven sons, has given him birth." Then Naomi took the child in her arms and cared for him. The women living there said, "Naomi has a son!" And they named him Obed. He was the father of Jess, the father of David. (Ruth 4:14–17, NIV)

Reflection

Naomi's story is the quintessential bittersweet story—kind of like a fairytale without the fairy. Her story has the happy ending we all love so much, but it is replete with tragedy, loss, hardships, and struggles. The gift of Naomi's story, particularly to women, is that we witness her making the necessary shift in life that causes her bitter story to end better. Naomi reminds women that our stories will always end better, regardless of how bitter they start, when we are open to life unfolding in ways we didn't plan.

Most of us have a planned for the kind of life we want to live. But life never goes completely according to plan. Life is full of surprises of varying kinds—good, bad, and ugly. Life never consults us about revisions it makes to our plan. But if we are open to flowing with the currents of life instead of being stuck to our own rigid plan, it may just lead us to experiencing lives we didn't know were possible.

Naomi's plan was to live a new life in a new country with her husband and two sons, but this plan came to a crushing halt. With the death of her husband and two sons, the life Naomi expected to live was no longer feasible. Naomi had to make adjustments as her life unfolded and her plan was altered. Naomi was bitter about her altered plan, as many of us would be (Ruth 1:20). When life doesn't pan out the way we hope, it's natural to mourn the loss of the life we hoped for. But like Naomi, we have to devise a new plan and look for new opportunities.

Naomi's story is encouraging for any woman who has ever lost a job, ran a business into the ground, experienced a painful divorce, or had her heart broken from a love that didn't last. She reminds women that good can grow from pain and that we possess the power to change the course of our lives by making sure we don't allow ourselves to stay stuck in the bitterness of a failed plan.

Naomi let go of the plan that died with her husband and sons and was open to new possibilities with her daughter-in-law. The new life Naomi embraced made her the great-great-grandmother to king David.

Our eyes really haven't seen, nor has it entered into our hearts, what God has in store for us. Being open to a different life can also mean opening ourselves to a better life. Flowing with the unpredictable currents of life can land us in good places.

Women who resist and reject the need to control every aspect of life are women who are destined to experience the fullness of what life has to offer.

Meditation Thought

Trust that your journey will not lead you astray. Be open to the Divine currents that are flowing in your life so that you may reach every destination and experience every opportunity that life has for you.

Affirmation Statement

I am open to life unfolding in ways I have not expected or anticipated.

Prayer

Dear Lord, this week remind me that the plans I design for my life are subject to the plan you have for me. Remind me to trust that my steps are ordered.

Journal Reflections

_____
_____
_____
_____
_____
_____
_____
_____
_____
_____
_____
_____
_____
_____
_____
_____
_____
_____
_____
_____
_____
_____

Week 36

Woman Caught in Adultery

Double Standard Denied

John 8:1-11

Scripture Focus

The teachers of the law and the Pharisees brought in a woman caught in the act of adultery. They made her stand before the group and said to Jesus, "Teacher, this woman was caught in the act of adultery. In the Law Moses commanded us to stone such women. Now what do you say?" They were using this question as a trap, in order to have a basis for accusing him. But Jesus bent down and started to write on the ground with his finger. When they kept on questioning him, he straightened up and said to them, "Let any one of you who is without sin be the first to throw a stone at her." Again he stooped down and wrote on the ground. At this, those who heard began to go away one at a time, the older ones first, until only Jesus was left, with the woman standing there. Jesus straightened up and asked her, "Woman where are they? Has no one condemned you?" "No one, sir," she said. Then neither do I condemn you," Jesus declared "Go and leave your life of sin." (John 8:3–11, NIV)

Reflection

No story more clearly exemplifies gender inequality like the story of the woman caught in adultery. Adultery, while a serious offense that should not be taken lightly, is one that is impossible for a woman commit alone. This woman's story is not only a reminder of how women are used as pawns in games some men play as they thirst for power and control, but it shows the unleveled playing field and the unfair treatment women often endure.

This story illustrates many modern-day stories where men get slaps on the wrist for their indiscretions while women suffer stiffer penalties. The double standard is clear when we consider how Clarence Thomas was rewarded with a seat on the Supreme Court and how the presidency was awarded to a sexual predator. We don't even allow Miss America or Miss USA to keep their titles when accusations of sexual indiscretions arise, but these men can climb to the pinnacle of success.

The woman caught in adultery, much like women today, was held to a higher standard by men who were unable to meet the mark themselves. Her story further exposes how Jesus will not tolerate an imbalanced and unfair treatment of women.

Not only does he refuse to condemn the woman, but he does something far more empowering for her and all women. He levels the playing field. He makes sure this woman isn't left with the idea that these men have some moral superiority over her because of their stations in life. He exposes them as frauds by bringing their transgressions into play. This woman is now able to see these men for who they are. She is able to give them the side-eye for their double standard in wanting her dead for her actions but giving themselves and the man she was caught with a pass.

Jesus doesn't excuse the woman's behavior, but he refuses to allow the gender imbalance, the double standard, and the inequality to go unchecked. In the tradition of Jesus, women must continue to check and call out the double standards and gender inequalities.

Women who stand up for themselves and other women for fair, equal, and just treatment are women who are assisting in bringing a kingdom-like reign to this world where women can live abundantly free.

Meditation Thought

"As women we must stand up for ourselves. As women we must stand up for each other. As women we must stand up for justice for all."—Michelle Obama

Affirmation Statement

I will not be held to a double standard. I will be seen and treated as an equal in every way.

Prayer

Dear Lord, this week help me to fight for fair and just treatment of women in the world and forever remember that a threat to justice anywhere is a threat to justice everywhere.

Journal Reflections

_____
_____
_____
_____
_____
_____
_____
_____
_____
_____
_____
_____
_____
_____
_____
_____
_____
_____
_____
_____

Week 37

Rebekah

Genesis 24:1-67

Scripture Focus

When they got up the next morning, he said, "Send me on my way to my master." But her brother and her mother replied, "Let the young woman remain with us ten days or so; then you may go." But he said to them, "Do not detain me, now that the Lord has granted success to my journey. Send me on my way so I may go to my master." Then they said, "Let's call the young woman and ask her about it." So they called Rebekah and asked her, "Will you go with this man?" "I will go," she said. So they sent her sister Rebekah on her way, along with her nurse and Abraham's servant and his men. (Gen. 24:54b–59, NIV)

Reflection

I n Rebekah's story we witness something rare. We witness a woman in a prominent biblical story who is invited to a seat at the table. Her story reminds women that plans and decisions that directly or indirectly impact the lives of women should never be made without consulting women. Women are reminded that we will never live our authentic and abundant lives without the decision-making power Rebekah displayed in her story.

In this rare occasion in the Bible, a decision about a woman's future wasn't made for her. It was made by her. When she was asked what she wanted, without hesitation, Rebekah made her desire clear. Rebekah considered the facts and was ready to make an informed decision that would benefit her.

Women in the Bible were rarely afforded the decision-making power Rebekah had. And centuries later, women are still struggling to make important decisions that impact our lives. When a new health-care bill was being crafted to replace the Affordable Care Act, not one woman was invited to sit at the table to give insight, input, and opinions about how this important piece of legislation might impact the lives of women; we were not invited to the table. Rebekah's story is a reminder to women who are still left out of important decisions how needed our voices are and how we must demand a seat at the table when it is being denied.

Shirley Chisholm, the first African American woman elected to the US Congress and the first African American candidate to run for president, encouraged us with her words: "If they don't give you a seat at the table, bring a folding chair." In other words, she reminds women to be at the tables of power by any means necessary to ensure our interests are not being overlooked. Representative Chisholm gave us this bold advice because she knew that old saying, "Those who aren't invited to the table are usually those who get served on the menu."

Collectively, a seat at the table allows women's voices to be heard and ensures that women's needs are front and center when important decisions are being made. Who better to share what women need than women? Whether it's collectively or personally, like Rebekah, women have to make sure we are directing our own destinies so that we end up in the God-intended places we were created to be in.

Women who show up at the table when it comes to important decisions that will impact on our future—invited or not—are women who are destined to live full and satisfied lives.

Meditation Thought

Be your own best champion. No one can articulate what's best for you like you.

Affirmation Statement

I will show up, stand up, and rise up on every front to ensure the full inclusion, respect, value, and consideration of women in every aspect of society. This I commit to do in service to myself and in service to other women.

Prayer

Dear Lord, this week help me to be assertive when it comes to decisions about my life, destiny, and future. Help me to not just show up but to be a powerful force articulating and ensuring my needs, wants, and desires are met. Help me remember that you have given me the responsibility of decision-making for my life.

Journal Reflections

_____

_____

_____

_____

_____

_____

_____

_____

_____

_____

_____

_____

_____

_____

_____

_____

_____

Week 38

Woman with the Issue of Blood

By Any Means Necessary

Mark 5:24-34

Scripture Focus

So Jesus went with him. A large crowd followed and pressed around him. And a woman was there who had been subject to bleeding for twelve years. She had suffered a great deal under the care of many doctors and had spent all she had, yet instead of getting better she grew worse. When she heard about Jesus, she came up behind him in the crowd and touched his cloak, because she thought, "If I just touch his clothes, I will be healed." (Mark 5:24–28, NIV)

Reflection

The woman with the issue of blood is an encouraging story of faith and healing, but it is also very much an encouraging story of relentless determination.

It is the story of a woman who would stop at nothing to secure the best possible future for herself. It is the story of a woman who had the intestinal fortitude to fight twelve long years for a life she knew was possible for her. She would pay a significant price for her new future, but she reminds women that no price is too high to pay to secure the futures God has for us.

This woman reminds us how important it is to give our very all to the things we desire most. She reminds women of the importance of investing in ourselves. She reminds us that there should be no guilt associated with pursuing goals, dreams, and desires you have for your own life. Paying every dime she had to doctors whose failed experiments made her worse didn't deter her. Failures on the journey to acquire our dreams are to be expected.

This woman persevered, even when it was against the rules of society, again proving to us that we have to go after the lives we believe is possible for us by any means necessary. Playing it safe won't assist us in living the lives we believe are possible. Taking risks is par for the course when pursuing life's dreams.

As a woman with an issue of blood, laws forbade her to be around and to touch people. This brought her to the fork in the road that many modern women face today. Women are often having to decide whether to follow the norms or take risks and chances that could possibly lead us to the lives we really want. Knowing that following the set expectations for women in her condition would not get her closer to what she wanted, she took a risk. She chose not to play it safe. She chose to live outside of the box of what others expected of her. And this is why she was healed.

Faith is taking risks. Faith is trusting and believing that still, small voice we hear in our spirit and following that voice in making decisions that are best for us. Just like this woman heard Jesus was near and pursued him until she connected in a way that changed her life, women today have to do the same thing by any means necessary if we want to live the lives we truly desire. We have to be as determined as she was. We have to invest in ourselves, take necessary risks, and be willing to ignore systems, people, and traditions that try confine us to where we are.

Women who are determined to live the lives they believe are possible for them by any means necessary are women who are destined to receive a confirming touch of approval from God that will affirm and change their lives forever. These are the women who will live abundantly free.

Meditation Thought

If you don't pursue the life you desire, you will live a mediocre existence.

Affirmation Statement

I am determined to pursue and live the abundantly blessed life I sense deep within my soul and spirit.

Prayer

Dear Lord, this week help me to let nothing keep me from the dreams, desires, and destiny for my life that I'm convinced you've placed in my heart and spirit. Help me take risks, invest in myself, and heed the internal voice within.

Journal Reflections

_____

_____

_____

_____

_____

_____

_____

_____

_____

_____

_____

_____

_____

_____

_____

_____

_____

_____

Keturah

Celebrate the Unsung

Genesis 25:1-6

Scripture Focus

Abraham took another wife, whose name was Keturah. She bore him Zimran, Jokshan, Medan, Midian, Ishbak and Shuah. (*Gen. 25:1–2, NIV*)

Reflection

Keturah is one of the unsung matriarchs in the Bible. She is one of the least known women in the Christian faith, but she's also one who is deserving of full recognition for her role in one of the most significant promises God ever made and fulfilled.

Keturah is the third wife of Abraham, and it is through her that God's promise to Abraham—that he would be the father of many nations and have as many offspring as there were stars in the sky—was fulfilled. Keturah played a significant role in this promise being fulfilled by giving birth to six of Abraham's sons. This is no small contribution, and for her contribution, Keturah is worth remembering.

Her story is a reminder of how women's contributions go unnoticed, are undervalued, and how women are unsung "sheroes" in a male-dominated world. It is also a reminder of how important it is for women to preserve the history and contributions other women make. When one woman's contribution is forgotten, we are all at risk of being forgotten. But when a spotlight is shown on one woman's accomplishment, it raises the capacity for more women to be seen. Every woman who is in a spotlight for some great accomplishment is there because some woman before her paved the way, and it is always appropriate to pay homage to women who've paved the way.

We have very little details about Keturah, but if Abraham was the father of many nations, that means Keturah was one of their mothers. Mothering nations is no small feat. As a mother of nations she is credited with influencing and shaping the lives of future leaders and nation builders. A woman selected by God to play a role of this magnitude had to be a woman of significance. While we may never know the extent of that significance, there is no refuting it.

Keturah is a reminder to women that while our stories may go unsung and our contributions go uncelebrated, it doesn't diminish their value. Keturah is the unsung "shero" reminding us of how God has been using women in significant ways throughout history. She is the reminder to women to never allow a lack of praise and acknowledgment to reduce our significance and our impact on this world. Her story should inspire women and compel us to sing our own praises and the praises of other women whose work and contributions go largely unnoticed. When the spotlight shines on one woman's accomplishments, it expands the visibility so that more women are seen.

When history tries to silence or diminish women's contributions, women have to stand up and shine the spotlight. Women must refuse to allow the significant contributions of women to go unsung.

Women who live out loud, refusing to allow their work and accomplishments and those of other women to be muted and unsung are ensuring that a right telling of history will be recorded. These women not only lay a foundation of freedom for themselves but for all women everywhere and those to come.

Meditation Thought

If she works and never gets credit, if she succeeds and is never acknowledged, and if she wins and there is no applause, it still counts.

Affirmation Statement

I am committed to shining as bright as I can, knowing that even if the world doesn't see my star, it doesn't diminish my ability to shine.

Prayer

Dear Lord, this week help me to remember that my contribution and the contributions of the women whose shoulders I stand are valuable whether they are widely known and celebrated or not. Help me to remember that good works can never be diminished.

Journal Reflections

_____
_____
_____
_____
_____
_____
_____
_____
_____
_____
_____
_____
_____
_____
_____
_____
_____
_____
_____
_____

Week 40

Peninnah

Toxic-Free Living

1 Samuel 1:1-7

Scripture Focus

He (Elkanah) had two wives, one was called Hannah and the other Peninnah. Peninnah had children, but Hannah had none. Year after year this man went up from his town to worship and sacrifice to the Lord Almighty at Shiloh, where Hophni and Phinehas, the two sons of Eli, were priest of the Lord. Whenever the day came for Elkanah to sacrifice, he would give portions of the meat to his wife Peninnah and to all her sons and daughters. But to Hannah he gave a double portion because he loved her, and the Lord had closed her womb. Because the Lord closed Hannah's womb, her rival kept provoking her in order to irritate her. This went on year after year. Whenever Hannah went up to the house of the Lord, her revival provoked her till she wept and would not eat. (1 Sam. 1:2–7, NIV)

125

Reflection

One of the things that prevents women from living the happy and free lives we desire is allowing the pains of life to poison us. This is the gift Peninnah's story gives us. Her story is a reminder to women how relationships that aren't nurturing can make us bitter and angry and hostile. It is a reminder of how unresolved resentment penetrates and poisons who we are.

Peninnah's story gives credence to the saying, "Hurt people hurt other people." At first glance we see her as a jealous, vindictive, and cruel woman, but if we look beyond the surface, we would probably find a wounded and hurt woman who has decided to share and spread her misery. Peninnah generally garners less of our sympathy and compassion because of the way she treats her rival Hannah, but a closer look at her story reveals that she is a neglected, unloved, undervalued woman, and therefore also deserving of our sympathy.

The misery Peninnah emits is not justifiable, but understandable. When women are forced to compete for the affection of one man, and he makes his preference clear, surely there will be some resentment. Perhaps her resentment went deeper because she was the wife who was solely responsible for her husband having heirs to carry on his name. Peninnah produced for her husband and was mother to his only children, yet she was loved less. She was unfairly treated. This was more than likely something that affected Peninnah deep within, but she had no outlet for her feelings. She had no right to divorce and no access to therapy to help reason through the pain of this ancient family dynamic that constantly made rivals out of women in the Bible. She was stuck in a relationship where she was emotionally undervalued, and with no grounds to stand against her husband, Hannah became the target of her pain.

Peninnah's mistreatment of Hannah is a result of a woman who has been deeply wounded and who has to live with those open wounds every day. Her story is a reminder of how unresolved pain destroys from within. It reminds women that harboring resentment and hate in your heart does nothing to harm the one you hate, but it destroys the one who hates.

Year after year, Peninnah held this vindictive grudge in attempts to make her rival feel the same hurt she felt. Perhaps she gained a sense of comfort seeing her rival cry, but it also meant that Peninnah had to constantly live in the hurt herself. When we hold on to pain and resentment, it imprisons us just as it did Peninnah. Misery loves company, which means we have to stay in the misery in order to make others miserable.

Peninnah reminds women that the poison of hate does more to keep us stuck and away from the life God intends us to live than it does to harm others.

Women who refuse to allow life's disappointments and pains to poison them will find true healing and peace. Internal healing and peace will always lead us to abundant free living.

Meditation Thought

How a person treats others is a reflection of how they feel inside.

Affirmation Statement

I will not use the hurt I experience as a weapon against others. I will not allow my present pain to poison my future.

Prayer

Dear Lord, this week help me to release any pain I maybe harboring so that I can live in your free and abundant grace.

Journal Reflections

Week 41

Tabitha/Dorcas

Ride-or-Die Sisterhood

Acts 9

Scripture Focus

In Joppa there was a disciple named Tabitha (in Greek her name is Dorcas); she was always doing good and helping the poor. About that time she became sick and died, and her body was washed and placed in an upstairs room. Lydda was near Joppa; so when the disciples heard that Peter was in Lydda, They sent two men to him and urged him, "Please come at once!" Peter went with them, and when he arrived he was taken upstairs to the room. All the widows stood around him, crying and showing him the robes and other clothing that Dorcas had made while she was still with them. Peter sent them all out of the room; then he got down on his knees and prayed. Turning toward the dead woman, he said, "Tabitha, get up." She opened her eyes, and seeing Peter she sat up. He took her by the hand and helped her to her feet. Then he called for the believers, especially the widows, and presented her to them alive. (Acts 9:36–41, NIV)

Reflection

When you have a sister circle of friends who refuse to let you die, who possess such defiant faith that they even tell death no, you must be journeying down the path of abundant free living. These ride-or-die widows possess the kind of faith and committed friendship that is needed to support every woman seeking to live free.

The widows of Acts chapter 9 are the exact kind of women most of would be blessed and fortunate to have in our sisterhood circle. We all would richly benefit from friends who possess the defiant faith these widows had—a faith that is so defiant that it literally rejects the death. Their rejection of her death is so defiant that they refused to bury her. They rejected Tabitha's harsh reality and believed that no matter how hopeless her situation was, it could get better.

Like Tabitha, when we have felt the sting of life's most devastating reality, and when we end up in dead-end, hopeless situations, we can only hope to have friends that will not only not give up on us, but who will spring into action to get us up and moving again.

As I read this passage, I couldn't help but wonder what inspired such friendship. I wondered what was it about Tabitha that compelled the widows to be so devoted to her that they refused to give up on her.

It was the mutuality of the friendship. These widows spoke about what Tabitha did for them when she was with them. They spoke of her always doing good and helping the poor. They had proof of her good deeds, showing clothing she made for them.

What made them not give up on Tabitha had to connect with who she was. When Tabitha was alive and the widows were in need, Tabitha covered them. Therefore, it was only fitting that they covered her when she was in need.

This story is a reminder to us to never give up on our sisters. When a woman is at a low point, it is sometimes that sister who comes along and demands that we get up and keep moving. It is those sisters who see that there is more to us and in us that can make the difference in whether we live our authentic abundant lives.

Women need sisters/friends and a strong sister circle who have the kind of relentless faith that refuses to give up, especially when it looks like all is lost. Sister circles full of women who have defiant faith are also full of women who are living abundantly free.

Mediation Statement

"A woman without her sisters is like a bird without wings."—Author Unknown

Affirmation

I am a fierce and defiant protector of the sisterhood. I believe all things are possible for women who believe.

Prayer

Dear Lord, this week help me to be the best sister and friend I can be to those women you have gifted to me.

Journal Reflections

Week 42

Moses's Mother

Seeing Is Believing

Exodus 2:1-10

Scripture Focus

Now a man of the house of Levi married a Levite woman, and she became pregnant and gave birth to a son. When she saw that he was a fine child, she hid him for three months. But when she could hide him no longer, she got a papyrus basket for him and coated it with tar and pitch. Then she placed the child in it and put in among the reeds along the bank of the Nile. (*Exod. 2:1–3 NIV*)

Reflection

A woman with Godly vision can see what is nearly impossible for others to see. A woman willing to respond to what she sees is a woman God can use to do extraordinary things—she is a woman who will live in authentic freedom!

Vision is everything for women who intend to live abundantly and authentically free. This is the kind of vision Moses's mother possessed. Moses's life was saved and liberation came to the people of Israel because of what Moses's mother was able to see in him. When Moses's mother "saw that Moses was a fine child," she was seeing beyond physical sight. She was seeing beyond how cute of a baby Moses was.

A quick study of this passage tells us that Moses's mother's reaction to "seeing" Moses was similar to God's reaction after God made all of creation. In the same way God looked at creation and "saw" that it was good and would fit the plan for which God created it, Moses's mother saw the same thing about what she created. She saw over and beyond what her physical sight could see. She saw more than her beautiful baby boy. She saw hope for what seemed like a hopeless future, and what she was able to see activated a faith in her that caused her to act with defiant faith.

She first hides Moses for three months against the Pharaoh's decree. With this action she becomes another woman who defies abusive, suppressive power. She rejects the decree Pharaoh instituted to kill all Hebrew boys. But when she could no longer hide Moses, when his cries got to loud for her to drown out, she made the riskiest move. She did what all the Hebrew mothers feared most. She exposed her son to the dangers of the Nile River. This took extreme, defiant, radical faith.

If you every wanted to know what radical faith is, Moses's mother's displays it wonderfully. I'm sure Moses's mother doubted whether the tar-pitched basket she made for Moses would keep him from the dangerous, treacherous Nile River. I'm sure she questioned if the basket could keep out the poisonous and sharp-toothed reptiles that made their homes in the river. But doubts and questions never stop a woman who has radical faith. This Levite woman who had a connection with God trusted that God was not only behind the vision she had about her baby boy, but that God would be the guiding force to ensure the vision was fulfilled.

Moses survived the journey down the river and the liberation this mother saw as she looked at her child came to be.

When we, like Moses's mother, are able to see what God sees, and when we are able to respond—even if it requires a radical response on our part—we afford ourselves a front-row seat to the unbelievable ways in which God works.

Women who able to fully trust what God shows them before any evidence of what they see actually appears are the women who play critical roles in God's Divine plan for the world. These women prove that they are living free.

Meditation Thought
Spiritual sight is a gateway to miracles.

Affirmation Statement
I am open to seeing more than what my physical sight can show me.

Prayer
Dear Lord, this week help me to see beyond the limitations of my physical sight. Help me to be open to seeing my circumstances through every available lens.

Journal Reflections

_____

_____

_____

_____

_____

_____

_____

_____

_____

_____

_____

_____

_____

_____

_____

_____

_____

Week 43

Ruth

Wrestle with the Word

Ruth 3:1-13

Scripture Focus

When Boaz finished eating and drinking and was in good spirits, he went over to lie down at the far end of the grain pile. Ruth approached quietly, uncovered his feet and lay down. (Ruth 3:7–8, NIV)

Reflection

Ruth's story is the story most known and referenced as a model for women who seek marriage, but Ruth's aggressive and nontraditional approach to securing the marriage is often what's not disclosed. What doesn't get translated about Ruth's story may have us clutching our pearls and cause us, from here on out, to do a more in-depth study of the scriptures so that our thinking, choices, and our faith is more informed. Ruth's story may just cause us to ask ourselves if we can really handle it when what the Bible actually says contradicts what we've been taught to believe. Women who seek to live in authentic freedom certainly can't live their without truth.

How Ruth is instructed by her mother-in-law to visit the man she is seeking to marry should make us raise our eyebrows. Ruth is instructed to bathe and perfume herself, wait until Boaz is drunk or tipsy, find where he is sleeping, and uncover his feet and lay down with him. What isn't often taught is that "uncovering his feet" is a Hebrew euphemism that really means uncovering his genitals. #ClutchingPearls

Another pearl-clutching moment is when Ruth's mother-in-law instructions Ruth to not make herself known to Boaz until after he has been drinking. We are all familiar with how the word "known" functions in the Bible. It's widely accepted that "known" is euphemism for sexual intimacy, and Ruth is instructed to make her self known to Boaz after he's in "good spirit."

Uncovering this new way of seeing Ruth may raise questions for us about traditional beliefs, which is a good thing. A faith that you can't wrestle with and question is a faith that is too small and limited. A god that you can put in a box, sum up, and fully explain is not the God most of us know. If we are honest, most of us are on a journey of figuring out faith as we walk blindly by it.

Seeing Ruth in a new light doesn't change the essence of who she is or the values we applaud in her. If anything, this new revelation humanizes her and invites us to have healthy conversations about sex and sexuality, topics that get too little attention in the church.

Women who are able to wrestle with the Word of God, even with its most uncomfortable and controversial topics, are women who will find the deep treasures of faith. Fearless women with fearless faith who aren't afraid to raise questions that lead to a more informed faith are women who are on the path to living free.

Meditation Thought

Never stop learning, because life never stops teaching.

Affirmation Statement

I am a woman unafraid to have my eyes widened to see more of the God I seek to know, love, and serve.

Prayer

Dear Lord, this week help me be open to what you would have me learn, know, and understand, even if it contradicts what I've already been taught. Help me to understand that if I'm open to truth and wisdom, you will not withhold these things from me.

Journal Reflections

_____
_____
_____
_____
_____
_____
_____
_____
_____
_____
_____
_____
_____
_____
_____
_____
_____
_____
_____
_____
_____
_____
_____
_____
_____
_____

Week 44

Mary (Mother of Jesus)

Let It Be

Luke 1:26-38

Scripture Focus

For nothing with God nothing shall be impossible. Then Mary said, "Behold the maidservant of the Lord! Let it be to me according to your word." Then the angel departed from her. (Luke 1:37–38, NKJV)

Reflection

Mary is one of the most well-known women in the Bible, and she reminds women to embrace everything God has for us, even the things that seem most unlikely. This young girl reminds grown women that when you are connected to the God who can do the impossible, it's OK to surrender, to let go of control, and relax into God's Divine plan for our lives.

This isn't easy for a lot of women. In this "make-it-happen" culture we live in, we've grown accustomed to figuring out and planning every detail to ensure our life's plan comes together. In this world where women are left behind and skipped over if we aren't aggressive and proactive about bringing our heart's desires into fruition, it's seems self-defeating to let go of control. Control ensures our goals are met. Control provides a sense of security. Control means minimizing unwelcomed outcomes. But control also signals that the onus for securing the life we want is squarely and solely on our shoulders, which limits space in our lives for God to do above what we think or imagine.

If we desire the unimaginable experiences of life that only God can manufacture, we have to discern the moments we are called to *do* something from the moments we are called to just *be*. Women—especially those who are driven, determined, and are used to having to fight for every inch of fulfillment in life—will benefit from knowing when to surrender and say, like Mary, "Let it be."

In Mary's wildest dreams she could have never put together a plan for herself like the one God had for her. The plan God had for Mary had never been done before. It had never been thought of before. She could have easily rejected God's plan by not surrendering, by being skeptical, or by believing that it was too wonderful a plan for some poor peasant girl. But Mary didn't stop to think if she was worthy. She didn't stop to think if Joseph would be OK with it. She didn't stop to think what people might say. Her response was a response of surrender—"Let it be." She welcomed God's plan, she embraced it, and she trusted God to work out all the details.

Mary's story is a reminder to women of the delicate dance strong, independent women must perfect between doing and being.

Women who understand that the fulfilling the lives we desire to live doesn't rest solely on our shoulders are women who are less stressed about their futures. These women have learned a healthy balance between what we can control and what we must surrender to God's control. These are women living in abundant and authentic freedom

Meditation Thought

There are moments in life when God expects us to do and moments God expects us to just be. There is no need to fear either of these moments because God is with us in both.

Affirmation Statement

I'm committed to perfecting and effortlessly mastering the dance between doing and being.

Prayer

Dear Lord, this week help me to discern when you are waiting on me to do all in my power to realize my hopes and dreams and help fulfill the plan you have for my life, and when I must be still and surrendered to receive what it is you are doing in my life. Grant me the wisdom to know the difference.

Journal Reflections

Daughters of Shallum

Women on the Wall

Nehemiah 3:1-12

Scripture Focus

And next to him was Shallum the son of Hallohesh, leader of half the district of Jerusalem; he and his daughters made repairs. (Neh. 3:12, NKJV)

Reflection

L ittle information is given about the daughters of Shallum. The little that is said of them, however, presents a little irony for contemporary women. The imagery of these women nestled between men working to rebuild the wall in Jerusalem is a modern American twist on the constant work women must do to tear down walls of exclusion in far too many fields of work.

Recently a Google employee penned a memo making baseless claims that women are not built for tech jobs. The male employee behind the memo stated as facts his bogus scientific belief that personality differences and low tolerance for stress were the reasons not many women hold leadership positions in the tech industry.

This sentiment about women is not just present in the tech field, it is also prevalent in others, including the field of ministry. The reason there are so few women pastors and many underpaid women in ministry is undergirded by the same unfounded belief of the man who penned the tech memo—a belief that a woman's biology prevents her from doing the job.

The daughters of Shallum bring to mind how women are underrepresented and undervalued in many fields and the ongoing work that must be done to address the unresolved issue of sexism. These daughters were just as capable and successful at restoring their piece of the wall as the men. And it's quite possible that if more women during this era had access and opportunity, we would be reading more names of women listed with the daughters of Shallum.

Access and opportunity is another issue that the daughters of Shallum help point out. Access and opportunity are what gives some women privileges over others. Perhaps the daughters of Shallum were the privileged women who had access and opportunity. Their father was leader of half the district of Jerusalem. Perhaps this gave his daughters some access to employment opportunities that other women didn't have.

This is the issue that birthed the womanist view, as women of color were for the most part left out of the feminist movement that catered to white women. Women of color and minorities suffer disproportionately from limited access and opportunities. In politics, entertainment, business, ministry, education, and so on, women of color and other minority groups are paid lower wages and have access to fewer opportunities than white women.

Whether the daughters of Shallum were privileged or not, they represent women who found space to do equal work alongside men. Their story reminds women of how long the battle has been waging for gender equality and how women must stay on the wall, building higher and hacking away until we reach and smash the proverbial glass ceiling.

Women who embody the feminist/womanist view of equality of the genders and equality for all women are women who are on the wall working to tear down strongholds of injustices against women and are rebuilding a world where women can thrive in every way. There is a lot of freedom in this kind of living.

Meditation Thought

Gender equality is not a woman's rights issue—it's a human rights issue. It affects us all.

Affirmation Statement

I will not accept a world that treats women as the lesser gender. I will work to change the world.

Prayer

Dear Lord, this week help me to work for a world that reflects the equality of both genders. Help me to spread a message of love and acceptance, where biological makeup does not grant superiority. Help me to fight for change where this understanding is not embraced.

Journal Reflections

_____
_____
_____
_____
_____
_____
_____
_____
_____
_____
_____
_____
_____
_____
_____
_____
_____

Elizabeth

Age Ain't Nothing but a Number

Luke 1:5-25

Scripture Focus

In the time of Herod king of Judea there was a priest named Zechariah, who belonged to the priestly division of Abijah; his wife Elizabeth was also a descendant of Aaron. Both of them were righteous in the sight of God, observing all the Lord's commands and decrees blamelessly. But they were childless because Elizabeth was not able to conceive, and they were both very old. (Luke 1:5–7, NIV)

But the angel said to him: "Do not be afraid, Zechariah; your prayer has been heard. Your wife Elizabeth will bear you a son and you are to call him John. (Luke 1:13, NIV)

Reflection

E lizabeth is another defiant woman of faith. She lands on our list because age limits didn't confine her nor prevent her from living the life she most desired. Her story encourages women who struggle with whether it's too late to fulfill a dream, accomplish a goal, or pursue a passion you've had for a while. Elizabeth speaks to women through the pages of the Gospel affirming for us that it's not too late, we're not too old, and we can still birth the unborn dreams of our hearts. She proves that age is just a number and it is no match for the God of a woman who believes she can still produce.

Elizabeth struggled with the issue of fertility that many women face today. Fertility is a painful issue that prevents too many women from the joys of biological motherhood. While Elizabeth's story gives hope and encouragement to women who are in the midst of the fertility struggle and who are believing for a favorable outcome, she also gives hope to women in general who have hit a certain milestone in age but have yet to accomplish a life goal.

Whether it's the dream of starting the business you've always wanted to start, writing a book, going back to school, playing an instrument, or even falling in love, Elizabeth reminds us that age is not a good enough reason to abandon that dream.

There is only one mandate for aging and that is to do it gracefully. Aging gracefully doesn't mean we give in or give up or hopes and dreams, it doesn't mean we are biding time, nor does it mean we've missed our opportunity. Aging is a gift. With age comes experience and wisdom, and it is quite possible that the dreams we've yet to fulfill will be even sweeter later in life because they will be sifted through the gifts of experience and wisdom.

Elizabeth ultimately reminds us that our time lines are in God's hands. She reminds us that a delay is not a denial and that we can still produce and give birth to every dream that lives in our hearts.

Women who embrace the adage that we get better with time are women who continue to produce and birth the desires of their hearts at every age, stage, and season of life. Women who believe it's never too late are women who are living abundantly free.

Meditation Thought

Live your life, do what makes you happy, and forget your age.

Affirmation Statement

I will embrace aging, as it does not determine my usefulness nor does it hinder my productivity.

Prayer

Dear Lord, this week help me to remember the beauty, grace, and gift of aging. At any given season of my life help me to not limit myself to what others believe is achievable or appropriate for me. Remind me that age is only a number.

Journal Reflections

Deborah

Balancing Act

Judges 4 and 5

Scripture Focus

At that time Deborah, a prophetess, wife of Lappidoth, was judging Israel. She used to sit under the palm of Deborah between Ramah and Bethel in the hill country of Ephraim; and the Israelites came up to her for judgment. (Judg. 4:4–5, NRSV)

Reflection

Do women have to sacrifice careers in order to have families? Do women have to sacrifice families in order to climb the corporate ladder? Can a woman be successful at home, in the office, and have time for herself? These are questions men rarely, if ever, have to answer. Men are expected to have careers and families, and neither is thought to suffer as a result of the other. But women are questioned about whether the same is possible. Can women be, do, and successfully balance more than one thing at a time? Deborah's response to the modern woman is yes!

Deborah, another defiant woman who judged Israel alongside a long list of men, is yelling to modern women from the ancient world that we can be, do, and have as much as we can balance. Deborah is the poster child for women who wear many hats, and she seems to do a great job of balancing it all. She is a prophetess, judge, wife, songwriter/poet, and a warrior. These are major roles that come with significant responsibilities.

As a prophetess, Deborah hears from God and speaks on God's behalf. As a judge, she rules and advises God's people. As a warrior, Deborah is on the front line of battles. As a wife, she plays a significant role in her family, and she still manages time to embrace her creativity as a songwriter/poet. Deborah is gifted and creative, fearless and wise—fulfilling every role and desire in her heart.

Deborah is no different from women today. Women today can fulfill our hearts desires, successfully wear all the hats God has assigned us, and successfully balance and juggle life. This means that we have to be intentional about what we put on our plates. Wise women like Deborah probably put only on their plates what is digestible. Juggling and balance many areas in life are possible when we don't tip our scales out of balance.

To balance it all effectively, support is needed. Deborah didn't go to war alone. She had Barak. She didn't manage her household alone. She had a husband. She wasn't an effective prophet and judge alone. She had God.

Deborah's story reminds women that we don't have to play Wonder Woman. A support system is a good and needed thing for women who are happiest when they are doing all God gifted them to do. Deborah reminds active, want-it-all-women to not go at it alone. Don't try to be a Superwoman; be a smart woman. Smart women have supportive networks and can balance more effectively.

Another thing that smart women do that Deborah also did—which more than likely made her juggle life more effectively—is make time for themselves. Deborah's writing was probably an outlet for her. She wrote a beautiful poem/song, and it was more than likely therapeutic for her with all the demanding responsibilities she had. Making time to rejuvenate and using a creative outlet to refresh is critical to a balanced life. All work and no play makes all of us dull women.

Women who are balanced are the happiest and most fulfilled women. These are women who refuse to live by the limited choices the world offers women. These are women who use tools and resources that help them shape life as it was meant to be for them. They are living authentically free.

Meditation Thought

"Happiness is not the goal, it is the by-product of a life well lived."—Eleanor Roosevelt

Affirmation Statement

I am determined to embrace everything God has for me and to live a balanced life that stems from my passion and purpose.

Prayer

Dear Lord, this week help me remember that I'm capable of more than the limitations the world places on me. Help me remember that my Divine connection, my support system, and self-care are the keys to keeping my life in perfect balance.

Journal Reflections

_____

_____

_____

_____

_____

_____

_____

_____

_____

_____

_____

_____

_____

Week 48

Esther

Esther 4-7

Scripture Focus

And Mordecai told them to answer Esther: "Do not think in your heart that you will escape in the king's palace any more than all the other Jews. For if you remain completely silent at this time, relief and deliverance will arise for the Jews from another place, but you and your father's house will perish. Yet who knows whether you have come to the kingdom for such a time as this?" Then Esther told them to reply to Mordecai: "Go, gather all the Jews who are present in Shushan, and fast for me; neither eat nor drink for three days, night or day. My maids and I will fast likewise. And so I will go to the king, which is against the law; and if I perish, I perish!" (Ester 4:13–26, NKJV)

Reflection

There comes a time in every woman's faith journey where we must learn the valuable lesson that everything isn't about us. One of the most precious gifts on our journey is when we discover that God's plan for us is larger than us and is intended to benefit more than just us. When we discover that God blesses us to be a blessing, and that God gives blessings to us in hope that God can give a blessing through us, it helps us align our lives, get in formation, and become God's agents of change in this world.

Esther's story is about a woman getting in formation and using her power, position, and influence to not just benefit her, but to get a win for her people. With a pivotal question posed to her from her uncle Mordecai, Esther was compelled to see her role and her position from a larger perspective. He asked her, "Who knows whether you have come to the kingdom for such a time as this?" This is a question all women should ask ourselves.

As God has strategically placed us in positions of leadership and authority or placed us in areas where we have the listening ear of someone in leadership who can influence change, we need to consider if we've been positioned for such a time as this. Whether we are teachers or CEOs, whether we are in politics or are business owners, whether we are stay-at-home moms on PTA boards or on the board of some Fortune 500 company, we have to ask ourselves how we can leverage our position so that God's greater good is achieved. This is what Esther did, and this is what it means to get in formation.

When it dawned on Esther that she could influence change to benefit and save her people, when she realized that she was perfectly positioned to not only stop the genocidal plan against her people, but uproot the threat altogether, she organized and went to work. She devised a plan that took great personal risk, determination, and a sense of fearlessness. She said, "If I perish, let me perish."

God can use women like Esther who are willing to put it all on the line. This also makes Esther a defiant woman of faith who went against the rules and put her life on the line to get a win for her people.

God can use women who are able to see their blessings and good fortune from a larger Divine perspective. God can and does use women who are willing to get in formation, line up their lives with God's plan, and bring a little more of the Kingdom of heaven on this earth.

Women who use their power, privilege, and influence to improve the lives of the others are a part of long and rich tradition of women who share in

God's mission to help the least, lost, and left behind. These women don't just have their own best interests in mind; they partner with God and use their available resources to support the mission and work of God's Kingdom. Abundant freedom belongs to fearless women like this.

Meditation Thought

"As you get, give. As you learn, teach."—Maya Angelou

Affirmation Statement

I am blessed to be a blessing. I will use my power, position, and influence in service to myself and others.

Prayer

Dear Lord, this week help me to remember the role I am to play in spreading love, joy, and peace in this world. Help me to always remember that you've strategically placed me in this world for such a time as this.

Journal Reflections

_____
_____
_____
_____
_____
_____
_____
_____
_____
_____
_____
_____
_____
_____
_____

Week 49

Eve

Embracing My Full Self

Genesis 3:1-24

Scripture Focus

> *Then the eyes of both of them were opened, and they knew that they were naked; and they sewed fig leaves together and made themselves coverings. And they heard the sound of the Lord God walking in the garden in the cool of the day, and Adam and his wife hid themselves from the presence of the Lord God among the trees of the garden.* (Gen. 3:7–8, NKJV)

Reflection

Eve's story doesn't directly speak to women about total self-acceptance, but in an indirect way she helps us wrestle with whether we are showing up in the world as our true, authentic selves or whether we are hiding. If we are able to see Eve's story beyond wrongfully villainizing her for the fall of humanity, we would see that she struggled to show up in the world unmasked and uncovered in the same way many women struggle today.

Eve was the epitome of a woman who showed up in the world as her naked, true, and authentic self. She was fully who God intended her to be, and she was totally comfortable in her nakedness. Eve felt no need to cover up and certainly no need to hide. But this all changed when she had a certain conversation that resulted in her seeing her self differently. This conversation was such a destructive force in Eve's life that it left her feeling shame and feeling as if something was wrong with her to the point that she no longer felt comfortable and confident in her own skin. From that point on, she felt the need to cover up and hide.

What happened to Eve is not uncommon. There are still voices today in our ears who are trying to convince us to change or cover up who we really are. There are voices that are much more comfortable when we conform and acquiesce to their ways of being in the world. Discerning these voices and thoroughly critiquing them will help us avoid Eve's fate. It will help us resist the need to cover and hide who we really are.

The best thing any woman can do for this world and the best gift we can give it is to show up in the fullness of who God created us to be. Diversity is a gift, and when we are all the same and we all try to fit one mode, it robs the world of the beauty God intended. Our differences are unique, and they give the world a depth of beauty.

Women who embrace the fullness of who they are and who are not afraid to show up in the world just the way God made them are women who make the world a brighter and more beautiful place.

Meditation Thought

The more comfortable we are in our own skin, the more uncomfortable we make people who aren't comfortable in theirs.

Affirmation Statement

I am unapologetically self-accepting, self-embracing, and self-loving. I am complete and enough just the way I am.

Prayer

Dear Lord, this week strengthen me to walk in the fullness of who you've created me to be. Help me to not dim my light, hide my gifts, limit my potential, or hinder what you intended me to be in this world.

Journal Reflections

Week 50

Rhoda

Nevertheless, She Persisted

Acts 12:1-19

Scripture Focus

As soon as he realized this, he went to the house of Mary, the mother of John whose other name was Mark, where many had gathered and were praying. When he knocked at the outer gate, a maid named Rhoda came to answer. On recognizing Peter's voice, she was so overjoyed that, instead of opening the gate, she ran in and announced that Peter was standing at the gate. They said to her, "You are out of your mind!" But she insisted that it was so. (Acts 12:12–15, NRSV)

Reflection

Rhoda is a reminder of the war women have been perpetually fighting to be heard, respected, and taken seriously. Women have been fighting to be heard for centuries, and if Rhoda's story reminds us of anything, it reminds us that women must continue to raise our voices until we are heard. Her story reminds women that we must insist our voices are heard and persist when they are not.

In great and small ways the voices, thoughts, opinions, and contributions of women have been rejected, ignored, and silenced. Whether in staff meetings across corporate America where a man's comment is accepted after a women who made the same comment earlier was rejected, or in some congregations where women are not allowed in pulpits to preach the Gospel, women are having to lace up the boxing gloves and get in the ring to fight for the right to be heard. It is a fight that does not discriminate and therefore it is a fight for all women, regardless of their socioeconomic background.

Rhoda was a maid, and perhaps her voice wasn't given credence because of her station in life, but these experiences happen to women of every station. Senator Elizabeth Warren's voice was ignored and interrupted as she tried to read a speech from Coretta Scott King at the confirmation hearing of the attorney general. Senator Warren's voice was devalued and dismissed just as Rhoda's was. This is a reminder to women that we are all in this fight together. We have to persist in this fight because the silencing of a woman's voice anywhere opens the door for the silencing of women's voices everywhere.

Just as Rhoda and Senator Warren persisted and insisted, all women must persist and insist. When they said to Rhoda, "You are out of your mind," she insisted. When they tried to silence Senator Warren, she persisted.

Rhoda knew she was right, and right should always demand to be heard. Rhoda reminds us that even when we are called crazy, even when we are made to feel like we are out of our minds, when we are made to feel like we are just being emotional, when we are made to fee like we out of or league or out of touch with reality, we have to persist and insist on being heard. We have to remember that we have valuable contributions, opinions, and thoughts, and we must be determined to not allow the value of our voices to be diminished.

Women who are determined to never allow their voices to be muzzled and muted are the fearless women the world needs. The fearless use of our voices will also pave the way to living out our authenticity so that we are as free as God intended.

Meditation Thought
Our silence on issues that are important is actually consent.

Affirmation Statement

I will use my voice, speak my truth, and reject the silencing of women.

Prayer

Dear Lord, this week help me to recognized when my voice is in jeopardy of being silenced, ignored, or diminished.

Journal Reflections

_____

_____

_____

_____

_____

_____

_____

_____

_____

_____

_____

_____

_____

_____

_____

_____

_____

_____

_____

_____

_____

_____

_____

_____

Week 51

Jehosheba

Village Power

2 Kings 11:1-3

Scripture Focus

When Athaliah the mother of Athaiah saw that her son was dead, she arose and destroyed all the royal heirs. But Jehosheba, the daughter of King Joram, sister of Ahaziah, took Joash the son of Athaziah, and stole him away from among the king's sons who were being murdered; and they hid him and his nurse in the bedroom, from Athaliah, so that he was not killed. So he was hidden wither in the house of the Lord for six years, while Athaliah reigned over the land. (2 Kings 11:1–3, NKJV)

Reflection

Jehosheba is literally a fearless sister who models for women what it means to be the village the next generation needs in order to thrive. She reminds aunts, godmothers, mentors, coaches, and all women who play a significant role in the life of a young person just how critical a role it can be. She is another defiant woman of faith who refuses to follow the rules and dictates of oppressive regimes.

Jehosheba is what a courageous and nurturing protector in the village looks like. She was the lifeline for her nephew, who would have otherwise been killed, never reaching his destiny. She was the aunt, the extended village who made sure her nephew fulfilled the potential for which he was destined. She made sure he became who he was meant to be.

When women step up like Jehosheba did to invest in young people and to support, protect, encourage, and nurture them, the payoff is often tremendous.

More than saving the life of her nephew, Jehosheba saved the lineage of King David and ensured that God's promise of the Messiah would be fulfilled.

Jehosheba's courageous story is a reminder to women of how the roles we play in the lives of young people can have significant impacts on our communities. Because Jehosheba acted as a courageous village elder for her nephew, he was able to fulfill his destiny as king in Judah.

Like Joash, there are young people who are destined to do great things, but they need encouragement, support, and at times, protection. Without the help of his aunt, his extended village, Joash's life would have been cut short.

Women who see potential in young people and take necessary measures to help them fulfill their potential strengthen the next generation and the community as a whole. When women invest in the lives of young people, we don't know the potential we are tapping into or the full return on the investment. Women who act as village elders are often fearless women of faith living free and ensuring the next generation has a chance to do the same.

Meditation Thought

Be the mentor, aunt, coach, and encourager to a young person that you wish you had when you were younger.

Affirmation Statement

I am committed to being a village elder and a fearless woman protecting the next generation of deserving youth.

Prayer

Dear Lord, this week help me to remember the importance of being a bridge to the next generation.

Journal Reflections

_____
_____
_____
_____
_____
_____
_____
_____
_____
_____
_____
_____
_____
_____
_____
_____
_____
_____
_____
_____
_____
_____
_____
_____

Shunammite Woman

It Is All Right

II Kings 4:8-37

Scripture Focus

The woman conceived and bore a son at that season, in due time, as Elisha had declared to her. When the child was older, he went out one day to his father among the reapers. He complained to his father, "Oh, my head, my head!" The father said to his servant, "Carry him to his mother." He carried him and brought him to his mother; the child sat on her lap until noon, and he died. She went up and laid him on the bed of the man of God, closed the door on him, and left. Then she called her husband, and said, "Send me on of the servants and one of the donkeys, so that I may quickly go to the man of God and come back again." He said, "Why go to him today? It is neither new moon nor Sabbath." She said, "It will be all right." Then she saddled the donkey and said to her servant, "Urge the animal on; do not hold back for me unless I tell you." So she set out, and came to the man of God at Mount Carmel. When the man of God saw her coming, he said to Gehazi his servant, "Look, there is the Shunammite woman;

Dr. Vanetta R. Rather

run at once to meet her, and say to her, 'Are you all right? Is your husband all right? Is the child all right?'" She answered, "It is all right." (2 Kings 4:17–27, NRSV)

Reflection

The Shunammite woman's story is a remarkable story of defiant faith. She reminds women of what it looks like to fully trust a God who gives life to the dead and calls those things that do not exist as though they did (Rom. 4:17). Her story is one that encourages and reminds women of the faith lens needed to view life, especially when the optics conflict with the desires of our hearts.

The Shunammite woman was delivered a devastating disruption in life. Her son unexpectedly died. But it is with his death that we are able to see her defiant faith—a faith so strong that it denied even death.

When her son dies, the Shunammite woman's defiant faith is undeniable. When asked about the well-being of her son she simply replied, "It is all right." She didn't say "It will be all right." She said, "It is all right." She possessed a faith that was convinced that God had the final say in all things, even over something as absolute as death. It was a faith that ignored reason. It was an irrational faith that ignored reality. And it is the kind of faith needed for women who seek to live lives that aren't dictated externally but rather guided internally.

The Shunammite woman's story is a reminder to women that we can't afford to be rational and reasonable when it comes to living the lives we believe God intended us to live. Living in freedom requires us to believe beyond what life sometimes shows us. It requires us to listen to and follow what the still, small, inner voices whispers to us.

The Shunammite didn't default to the option of mourning and burying her son. This wasn't a reasonable option for her. The only outcome she saw was her son living. She spoke it, believed it, and took steps to ensure it. And to live the lives we desire, we must do the same.

Even as this woman held the lifeless body of her dead son in her arms, as she felt his body temperature lose its warmth, it wasn't enough to convince her

162

that all was lost. She still believed. She was convinced that her son was all right, and she never stopped believing until her words matched her son's reality.

The Shunammite woman reminds us that life and death are in the power of the tongue and that even seemingly dead dreams can be resurrected if we speak and act as she did. Her faith was an active and defiant faith that didn't just speak, didn't just believe, but actively worked toward the desired outcome.

Women who will live lives they believe God intended must possess a defiant, active faith! This is a faith that believes—even when our hopes, dreams, and desires appear dead—that it's still all right!

Women who walk by faith and not by sight are women who will find themselves living authentically free.

Meditation Thought

Seeing life through the lens of faith will help guide you to Divine places meant for you.

Affirmation Statement

I will embrace and accept in life only what I'm certain is a part of God's plan for my life.

Prayer

Dear Lord, this week remind me that living by faith may mean that I see what others may never see. In those moments, help me to trust my faith sense more than what makes rational sense.

Journal Reflections

_____

_____

_____

_____

_____

_____

_____

_____

_____

_____

About the Author

Dr. Vanetta Rather is a preacher, teacher, author, and a fierce advocate for women and girls. She is the founder of My Sister My Seed, Inc., a 501c3 nonprofit with a mission to *"Create a safer and a more just world for women and girls."*

Born in Newport News, Virginia, and raised in the inner city of southeast Washington, DC, Dr. Rather knows what it's like to experience both love and lack. She is proud of the roots from which she hails, as they have helped give her the self-determination to persevere and pursue purpose with passion. Her desire to live her purpose and to help others do the same is a direct reflection of the family and community in which she was raised.

Dr. Rather graduated magna cum laude from Springfield College in Springfield, Massachusetts, with a Bachelor of Science in Human Service. She went on to earn a Master of Divinity and later a Doctor of Ministry with a concentration in preaching in the twenty-first century from the Wesley Theological Seminary in Washington, DC. She is very passionate about preaching, and she uses her passion to spread an empowering message of self-love, self-worth, and value to all, especially women and girls who are too often marginalized, left out, and left behind.

Her work speaks for itself and has garnered Dr. Rather awards and acknowledgements including the Eboné Image Award from the National Coalition of One Hundred Black Women, Inc., as well as an acknowledgment from the former lieutenant governor of the state of Maryland, Anthony G. Brown.

Dr. Rather penned *All the Single Ladies: Modern Single & Faithful*, a book that encourages and seeks to remind women that they can embrace this modern culture and remain committed to an ageless faith. Dr. Rather desires women of faith to break the bonds of cultural and faith traditions that hinder women and keep them from the abundant life God called them to live.

Using her advocacy work and her skills as a homiletician, Dr. Rather is extremely grateful and honored to fulfill her life's mission to build the Kingdom of God on earth as it is in heaven.

Dr. Rather serves as an associate minister at the Mount Olive Baptist Church in Arlington, Virginia.

Made in the USA
Middletown, DE
14 February 2023

24788085R00104